The Church

Past

Present

and

Future

Dr. Stanley K. McCrary

OAKES BOOKS

A Full Circle Publishing Company

Copyright©2013 by Oakes Books

ISBN 978-0-9842649-5-7

All rights reserved except for use in any review for newspaper, magazine, or journal. The reproduction or utilization of this work in whole or in part, in any form, now known or hereafter invented is forbidden without the written permission of the publisher, Oakes Books.

Note: All scripture references are from the King James Version of the Bible unless otherwise stated.

Oakes Books and Publishing
620 18th Ave E. Ste. 15
Seattle, WA 98112
(253) 228-9672

Cover Design by *Scribes Freelance*
www.scribesfreelance.com

Acknowledgments

First and foremost, I thank God for making all of this possible. If it had not been for the Lord on my side, tell me where would I be? (Lost)

I want to thank my beautiful wife, Surenell, for all her comfort and support. Thank you for being there for me.

To my Mt Pleasant Baptist Church Family: Thank you for allowing me to be your pastor and teacher. You allowed me to put this book into action.

To my fellow preachers and pastors I thank you for your guidance and prayers.

A very special thank you to Mrs. Geraldine Shambry for not allowing me to submit this until **she** told me it was "ready".

To my publisher, Cassandra Oakes, you're the best! Thank you for all your help, suggestions, ideas… everything!

Finally to my readers: Thank you for picking up this book and learning about this place we call "church". May it be a blessing to you as you read it as it was to me as I wrote it.

To God Be the Glory!

Table of Contents

Chapter		Page
	Introduction	6

Part I
The Past (The History of the Church)

1	What is the Church?	8
2	Jesus: The Church's Architect	24
3	The First Church	46

Part II
The Present (The Church of Today)

4	What happened to the Church?	57
5	Wolves in Sheep's Clothing	92
6	The Mega Church	128
7	Church Membership: Required or Optional?	150
8	Denominations	165

Part III
The Future (The Church of Tomorrow)

9	The Emerging Church	194
10	Church Theology	216
	Works Cited	238

The Church

Past

Present

and Future

Introduction

Ask ten people to give you a definition for the word "Church" and you may get ten different answers. Why is this? It could be due to the vast array of churches that exist today. Where did the church come from? Who built it? Why do we go to church?

This project will attempt to provide a theological insight into the original purpose and mission of the church. It begins by looking to the past and reviewing the history of the church. The concept of the universal church and the local church will be explored in order to provide the proper meaning. Once this foundation is laid, a closer look at the church of today will be better appreciated. Subjects such as **Denomination**, **Membership**, and the ever growing phenomenon of the **Mega-Church** will be examined.

Finally, there is a look ahead to the future to see where the church of tomorrow is going. The "**Emerging Church**", which is growing in popularity, will be dissected to uncover just what it is and why many are being drawn to it.

After all of these areas are observed a theological understanding of what the church is will be obtained. Applicable sermons are added for contextual relevance. This is the mission of this work.

As the writer of Proverbs informs us in chapter 4 verse 7:

"Wisdom is the principal thing; therefore get wisdom: and with all thy getting get understanding."

Note: All scripture references are from the King James Version of the Bible unless otherwise stated.

Part I

The Past

The History of the Church

Chapter One

What is the Church?

The term "Church" is used by Christians in two different but closely related ways. It can refer to all of Jesus' followers viewed as a community. It can also refer to specific institutions, either the local congregation or a national or international body. It can even be used to refer to the building in which they meet.

The church is important, because God does not save people in isolation. An important part of what needs to be restored is our relationship with other people. That can only be done by the community as a whole.

The church is also the group with which we worship. As such it has the responsibility to preach the Word of God and to administrator the sacraments. These are critical elements in maintaining our fellowship with God and each other as Christ left these two ordinances for the church to do.

The church also has a responsibility to encourage its members to make spiritual progress, and to show their faith by their behavior, both through their ethics and their good works. This responsibility includes administering brotherly correction when someone errs. Traditionally the church has felt a responsibility to discipline, and if necessary exclude, members whose public lives are not in keeping with the message of

Christianity. Not all churches are equally careful about carrying this out. It is in fact one of the more difficult responsibilities to get right. It is very, very easy for church discipline to lead to self-righteousness and intolerance.

The English word "Church" is believed to be a derivative of the Greek word *kuriakos,* meaning "of or belonging to the Lord." It is used to translate the Greek word *ekklesia,* which occurs 77 times in the New Testament, with all but four occurrences (Acts 7:38; 19:32, 39, 41) referring to God's people of the new covenant. *Ekklesia* is a compound formed from the Greek preposition *ek* (meaning "out of") and the Greek noun *klesis* (meaning "a calling"). Therefore the "Church" is literally "Who hath delivered us from the power of darkness, and hath translated us into the kingdom of his dear Son (Col. 1:13). This is not to infer that the church and God are the same, but rather to illustrate that the "church" is made up of those who were once in darkness and are now walking in the light of Jesus.

It is noteworthy that Jesus used the word "church" only three times in two different passages, but His usage of the word illustrates the two basic senses in which it is used in the New Testament. When He said, "I will build my church" (Matt. 16:18), He used the word in the *universal* sense, including all of His disciples throughout the world. When He spoke of brothers disagreeing and the matter being ultimately taken to the church (Matt. 18:15-17), He used the word in the *local* sense, referring to a body of His disciples within a particular geographical area who come together for purposes of work and worship.

Christian Understanding of 'Church'

Ecclesia (or **Ekklesia**) in Christian Theology denotes both a particular body of faithful people, and the whole body of the faithful. Latin *ecclesia*, from Greek *ekklesia* had an original meaning of "assembly, congregation, council", and literally "convocation".

More narrowly, it may signify the whole body of Christian faithful, including not merely the members of the church who are alive on earth but those, too, who have fallen asleep in Christ, and as such form part of the communion of saints, are also to be considered the Body of Christ. Some churches therefore describe the church as being composed of the Church Militant and the Church Triumphant (being those Christians on Earth and in Heaven; respectively.)

In Catholic theology, there is also the Church Suffering comprising those in purgatory. The Christian family, the most basic unit of church life, is sometimes called the domestic church.

Finally, "The Church" may sometimes be used, especially in Catholic theology, to designate those who exercise the office of teaching and ruling the faithful, the Ecclesia Docens, or again; the governed as distinguished from their pastors, the Ecclesia Discens.

Some theologians (e.g. Baptists, Methodists) accept the local sense as the only valid application of the term "church", in so doing rejecting wholesale the notion of a universal ("catholic") church. They believe that all uses of the Greek word "ekklesia" in the New Testament are speaking of either a particular local group or of the notion of "church" in the abstract, and never of a single, worldwide church. To better understand this, a closer observation of the major differences between the Catholic and Protestant faiths is in order.

The Catholic Church

How is it organized?

By the end of the 1st Century, authority in the church centered on Bishops who were seen as successors to the Apostles. Bishops are consecrated by other Bishops (normally at least three). Using this principle every Bishop can trace their authority back through an unbroken line of consecrations to the Apostles, and then Christ. This is referred to as the "Apostolic succession".

Currently Bishops are normally responsible for a city and the surrounding territory. Bishops have several different kinds of authority and responsibility.

- They have the responsibility for maintaining proper doctrine in the area for which they are responsible.
- They are responsible for the proper conduct of the sacraments. They normally conduct certain sacraments (e.g. confirmation) personally.
- They delegate authority to Priests.

As the early churches grew certain bishops developed greater prestige than others. This was often because of the history or role of their cities. The bishops of these key cities have special leadership responsibilities.

In the East, they are referred to as "Patriarchs". In the West, the bishop of Rome is regarded as the Preeminent Bishop. He is normally referred to as the "Pope".

The Pope has two conceptually separate roles:

- He is the patriarch of the Roman Catholic Church. As such, he is ultimately responsible for everything that happens in that communion. He makes key appointments and decisions, and can review any action. In the Catholic tradition, the Pope is also seen as the spokesman for the Church as a whole. He has a special responsibility for maintaining proper doctrine and morals. As part of this responsibility, he or his representative chairs all ecumenical councils. He may also make authoritative doctrinal decisions on his own authority (which comes from Christ).
- The Pope has leadership responsibilities over churches other than the Roman Catholic Church, i.e. churches of which he is not the patriarch. In such churches the Pope would not directly govern, but they would still be subject to his overall doctrinal leadership. There are a few Eastern churches that accept this concept. However the major Orthodox churches do not accept the Pope's idea of universal leadership. Many of them would accept him in some role of spokesman. But generally they do not accept papal infallibility, and they also believe that he has often attempted to make decisions for other churches that are properly the responsibility of their own leadership.

The Catholic and Orthodox traditions emphasize continuity in doctrine and in worship. The bishops have a primary role as carriers of the tradition. They are expected to hold to the original faith as given to the Apostles, and also to work together and with the Pope (or all the patriarchs, for the Orthodox) to maintain common doctrine and practice throughout the Church.

The office of Priest developed slightly later. Originally they were seen primarily as assistants to the bishop. Priests are typically responsible for an individual congregation or church. This isn't exact: Larger churches may have more than one, and sometimes a single priest may have more than one church. The priest is responsible for guiding the life of the congregation, and for conducting most normal sacraments. Priests are ordained by Bishops.

Certain of the sacraments (e.g. communion) may only be performed by a priest or bishop. This is not just an issue of who has permission to do it. At ordination, a priest receives spiritual authority. Without that authority, the transformation of the bread and wine into Christ's body and blood in communion will not occur.

How is it authorized?

Catholics believe that the Church was given authority by Christ to make decisions. These include both doctrinal and moral issues. This authority is lodged primarily in the bishops and the Pope. In appropriate circumstances, their decisions can be infallible. The teaching authority of the Church is referred to as the "magisterium". Catholic writers sometimes distinguish between the "ordinary magisterium" and infallible teaching.

The ordinary magisterium is the teaching responsibility as carried out through ordinary preaching and catechesis, as well as through specific pronouncements such as encyclicals and pastoral letters. Although teachings of the ordinary magisterium are not exactly infallible, they are part of a process that is guided by the Holy Spirit. Thus it is expected that Catholics will receive such teaching as authoritative.

Catholics also believe that is possible for the Church to make infallible decisions. There are two ways of doing this: an ecumenical council, and a direct papal decision. When an ecumenical council makes doctrinal decisions, in union with the pope, they may be infallible. In addition to this, the pope himself may make infallible decisions.

The concept of papal infallibility is often misunderstood. It does not mean that everything the Pope does is perfect. Many popes have been seriously flawed. Rather, the belief is that the Holy Spirit guides the Church in such a way that when the Pope makes certain solemn pronouncements in the areas of faith and morals, those pronouncements are infallible. The Pope has this role because he is the one who speaks for the Church as a whole.

This class of pronouncement is referred to as "ex cathedra" ("from the chair", i.e. the official bishop's throne). All Catholic scholars agree that there have been two infallible pronouncements. Many have longer lists, up to about 20 items. (Note that there is not an infallible list of infallible pronouncements.) These are in addition to documents produced by church councils. They may also be regarded as infallible. But they are not specifically based on exercise of papal infallibility.

Historically, Catholics have been very concerned about maintaining high moral standards among their members. Members are required to confess their sins to a priest. The priest is expected to provide both spiritual and ethical guidance.

Summation

For the Catholic tradition the key marks of the Church are defined by four phrases used in the Apostles ' Creed:
- It is the one, holy, Catholic, and Apostolic church. The term "Catholic" means "universal". The Church is universal, and it is one. Its doctrines can be traced to the Apostles.

The Protestant Church

How is it organized?

In general Protestants vary a lot in the way that their churches are organized. There is far more variation here than in beliefs and practices. Many Protestants would say that a single scheme of church organization is not described in the Bible, although certain guiding principles are given. This leaves individual churches free to adopt different patterns.

Protestant churches may be classified on a spectrum with "connectional" churches on one end and "congregational" churches on the other end. In connectional churches, there are national and regional bodies, which have a good deal of authority. Quite often higher-level bodies review what lower bodies do, and can take action to overrule them.

In the Presbyterian Church, it is possible for a Presbytery to unseat the Session (governing board) of a local church, and appoint its own governing board. This is typically done in a situation where there is a conflict within the local church that it does not appear the church can handle for itself.

In some connectional churches (e.g. the Methodists), pastors are assigned to local churches by a central authority (in this case the bishop).

In congregational churches, each congregation is independent. They call their own pastor and make their own decisions. No higher level body can intervene. Many congregational churches still have national and regional organizations. They coordinate programs that require cooperation beyond a single congregation, e.g. sending missionaries, preparing Sunday School curriculum material, and running seminaries (colleges for training pastors). However a few traditions (particularly more conservative portions of the Church of Christ) do not believe that any higher level body is permissible, even for voluntary cooperation. There is quite a variety of patterns between these two extremes.

Protestant Churches base their organization on a few common patterns. Many Protestant churches have bishops. Except in a few cases (Anglicans, Lutherans in Scandinavia), these bishops do not have the Apostolic succession. They are simply elected by the church as leaders. Thus these bishops are sometimes called "titular bishops", to distinguish them from canonical bishops that do have the Apostolic succession. In general the Lutheran and Methodist traditions include bishops. Since the Pentecostal and Holiness churches are developments from the Methodists, they often have bishops as well.

Almost all Protestant churches have elected leaders. Normally there is a governing board of some sort for the local church. For connectional denominations, the national and regional levels also have elected groups that function more or less as legislatures. (The U.S. government is modeled after Presbyterian Church government.) Clergy and bishops (if any) normally serve in these bodies, either as part of a single body or (in a few churches) as a separate "house", like the Senate and House of Representatives.

Protestant Churches try to base their church organization on the Bible. While the Bible doesn't give a specific plan of government, several offices are referred to in governing. These include Deacon, Elder, Bishop, and Apostle. Not all churches use all offices. Most churches believe that the office of apostle applied only to Christ's followers, and that there are no longer apostles. Some identify two offices, or split a single office into two variants.

In the Catholic and Orthodox traditions, there is a clear distinction between "Lay People" and "Clergy". Clergy have been ordained. Ordination is a sacrament, which imparts a permanent metaphysical mark on the soul. Clergy include bishops and priests, and in some sense also permanent deacons.

For Protestants, this sort of distinction is not as clear. Protestants do have leaders that more or less correspond to priests. They are commonly called pastors or ministers, though a few Protestant groups use the term "priest". Pastors commonly have special education, either a graduate degree or training at a Bible college. They are commonly full-time. They are normally ordained. That means that they are set apart in a special ceremony, and that they have the authority to celebrate baptism and communion.

However for Protestants, ordination doesn't confer any special metaphysical powers. The fact that only pastors lead in a communion service is a matter of church order and not that only they have the power to make bread and wine change into Christ's body and blood, (as in the Catholic tradition).

Protestants often use the term "Lay" to refer to everyone other than pastors, although it's not clear to me that the lay/clergy distinction is actually consistent with Protestant theory. In all Protestant churches that

I know, each congregation has lay leaders that serve alongside the pastors. Their exact relationship varies by denomination. However the lay leadership tends to have a stronger role for Protestant churches than for Catholic ones.

The exact set of lay leaders varies. However one common pattern has Deacons and Elders. In this pattern the deacons are typically responsible for charitable activities, and elders for policy decisions. However not all churches use both deacons and elders.

In the Reformed tradition (which includes Presbyterians), all leaders are ordained. Since the distinction between lay and clergy was traditionally ordination, in some sense this means that Reformed churches have no lay leadership. However for most purposes Reformed deacons and elders are thought of as lay:

- They are not full-time positions.
- The positions tend to rotate among the active members of the congregation.[1]

Some also note the distinction between the word 'ekklesia' (or 'ecclesia') from the word "Church". The 'ekklesia' represents the congregation or living body of believers in Christ, as compared to the "church" which more represents the religious institution or organization (e.g. Catholic Church). The 'ekklesia' appears to be what Christ was referring to in the New Testament when he said 'Upon this Rock I will build my ekklesia, and the gates of hell shall not prevail against it' (Matt. 16:18). The reference here is the original Greek meaning of the 'ekklesia'[2].

Church History

Relevant for Modern Christianity

Church History on the surface seems irrelevant to 21st Century Christianity. Many Christians are more concerned with where the church is going instead of remembering where it came from. There are churches that appear to be in competition with the secular world to draw more people into the sanctuary than to Christ. However, **Christianity**, unlike any other religion, is deeply rooted in history.

Central to the Christian faith is the fact that God came to earth as a man -- **Jesus Christ**. He lived, loved and taught among humanity over 2000 years ago. The historical reality of His sacrifice, burial and resurrection is the cornerstone of the **Christian faith**. The Bible is not a fairy tale but a divinely inspired historical record of God's plan of redemption for a world lost in sin. It was written by men who were inspired by the Holy Spirit. When one studies church history he is allowed to see the hand of God at work amidst the strife, transgression and glory of man's ways.

The Importance of Church History

Church history is vital to our understanding of the institution of the Christian church. Much is to be learned from the events between the time of the apostles and the present. In 1 Corinthians 10:1-13, the apostle Paul exhorts the Corinthian church to learn from the examples of Israel's past, lest they make the same mistakes. Like the history of ancient Israel, the history of the Christian church is to be remembered and studied.

For instance, many who are skeptical of the Christian faith often associate Christianity with the violence and imperialism of the crusades. But an objective look at church history will show that the crusades happened at a time when the papacy was a political institution corrupted by power and greed. The crusades took advantage of Christianity and had nothing to do with the underlying gospel of grace.

Today, our culture is often confronted with new and bizarre religious philosophies, some of which present themselves under the banner of Christianity. This is nothing new. History is littered with heresies that have tried to infiltrate the church, including false ideas such as Gnosticism.

Understanding Christian doctrine in light of church history helps one to separate fiction and fads from the facts and doctrine of the true Christian faith.

Church History -- *A Simple Chronology*

Church history is rather complex, but an understanding of the basics is very worthwhile. The following is a simple chronology of church history adapted from Bruce Shelley's <u>Church History in Plain Language</u>[3]:

(30-70 AD) The Time of Jesus and the Apostles
* The death and resurrection of Christ.

* The Christian faith is birthed and the gospel of grace is preached.

(70-312) The Age of Catholic Christianity

* The spread of the Christian faith; martyrdom of the early believers.
* Early heresies sprouted; first church councils and the canonizing of scripture.

(312-590) The Age of the Christian Empire

* Constantine declares Christianity the official religion of the Roman Empire; Age of great councils.
* Christianity became a faith for the masses; start of Monasticism.

(590-1517) The Middle Ages

* The fall of Rome and the Byzantine Empire.
* Benedictine monks deployed as missionaries; the Pope becomes the "ruler" of the church.
* The crusades: The church gains the world but loses its soul.

(1517-1648) The Age of Reformation

* Martin Luther and the protestant movement.
* The start of denominationalism - Examples: Lutheran, Reformed, Anabaptist and Anglican.
* The papacy loses its power and influence.

(1648-1789) The Age of Reason and Revival

* Secularism -- The mind becomes god; people begin to ask, "Who needs God?"
* Revivals such as Pietism, Methodism and the Great Awakening seek to restore God to public life.

(1789-1914) The Age of Progress

* The message of Christ is carried to distant lands, but the faith continues to leave public life.

* Pluralistic and totalitarian societies see no relevance for Christianity.

(1912-current) The Age of Ideologies...

Who designed the church? Who built it? Who paid for it? These questions will be answered in the following chapter.

Chapter Two

Jesus

The Church's Architect

Jesus Christ is the designer and builder of the church, for he said, "I will build my church … " (Matt. 16:18). For this reason it bears His name (Rom. 16:16). No church, which was founded by men or bears the name of a man (as well as humanly devised names), can ever have been the church founded by Christ. The foundation of the church is Jesus Christ in His divine nature as the Son of God (Matt. 16:16). There is no stronger or surer foundation on which the church may be built, and any church, which is established upon a different principle, does not have that distinctive, essential feature which marks a true church of Christ. It is quite evident that the church began on the first day of Pentecost following Jesus' ascension.

The Church Was Purposed by God from Eternity

The church played a major role in the eternal purpose of God, thereby demonstrating God's wisdom (Eph. 3:10-11). The church is not a last-minute substitute. A beautiful painting reveals the skill of the artist. A powerful rocket reveals the wisdom of its makers. So the church reveals the wisdom of God as part of His eternal purpose. To say the church is not essential is to say that the eternal purpose of God is not essential. The church was designed by God.

The Purpose for the Church
I Samuel 21:1-9

Introduction

What is the purpose for the church? Is it a place where we come to worship God? Is it a building that we proudly show our visitors and friends? Is it a place where we come to hear from heaven? Just why do YOU come to church? In our text today we find David on the run from Saul. Saul is after David and wants to kill him. David flees to Nob and enters the temple. There he finds two things; he feeds with **Bread**, he finds a **Blade**, and I add the third … he has **Belief**.

Prologue

I Samuel 21: 1-2

(*This conversation is based on a lie.*)

Here David did not behave like himself. He told Ahimelech a gross untruth, that Saul had ordered him business to dispatch, that his attendants were dismissed to such a place, and that he was charged to observe secrecy and therefore durst not communicate it, no, not to the priest himself.

This was all false. What shall we say to this? The scripture does not conceal it, and we dare not justify it. It was ill done, and proved of bad consequence; for it occasioned the death of the priests of the Lord, as David reflected upon it afterwards with regret, (*1 Sam 22:22.*)

It was needless for him thus to dissemble with the priest, for we may suppose that, if he had told him the truth, he would have sheltered and relieved him as readily as Samuel did, and would have known the better how to advise him and enquire of God for him. People should be free with their faithful ministers.

David was a man of great faith and courage, and yet now both failed him, and he fell thus foully through fear and cowardice, and both owing to the weakness of his faith. Had he trusted God aright, he would not have used such a sorry sinful shift as this for his own preservation. It is written, not for our imitation, no, not in the greatest straits, but for our admonition. Let him that thinks he stands take heed lest he fall; and let us all pray daily, Lord, lead us not into temptation.

Bread

I Samuel 21: 3

David was hungry. He asks the priest for some food. The priest tells him that the only food they have is the *shew* bread or the bread that is offered up before God.

- "The pure table" (***Lev 24:6***), both because of its unalloyed gold and because of the "pure offering" on it (***Mal 1:11***). The table stood in the holy place on the N. side (***Ex 26:35***). The 12 cakes of unleavened bread, arranged in two piles, with a golden cup of frankincense on each (Josephus Ant. 3:10, section 7), were renewed every Sabbath, and the stale loaves given to the priests.

They represented the 12 tribes before Jehovah perpetually, (***Rev 21:12***) in token that He was always graciously accepting His people and their good works, for whom atonement had been made by the victims on the altar outside.

We also come to church for bread.

John 6:35

"And Jesus said unto them, I am the bread of life: he that cometh to me shall never hunger; and he that believeth on me shall never thirst."

John 6:48,

"I am that bread of life."

The church is a place for us to come and receive the Word of God from God. It's not a place to hold any program that does not honor God. The church is a place for healing. You should not come to church pretending and expect God to be straight with you and you're not being straight with God.

Blade
I Samuel 21:8

David asks for a weapon. He lies again saying that he left in a hurry to do the king's business. The priest tells David that the sword that he used to kill Goliath is there and that David can have it.

We come to church to get our blade, our sword which the Bible tells us in ***Eph 6: 17b***, ***"and the sword of Spirit, which is the word of God."***

You need the Word of God to be your weapon. When we leave the church we go into the world to seek the lost. You're going to need your weapon!

Belief

I John 3:23

"And this is his commandment, That we should believe on the name of his Son Jesus Christ, and love one another, as he gave us commandment."

Luke 14:23, "And the lord said unto the servant, Go out into the highways and hedges, and compel them to come in, that my house may be filled."

If we want the church to grow we must go out and find them! If we sit in here and wait for the lost, the un-churched, to come, we'll still be here waiting on Jesus. Jesus tells us to go out and find them! So, let's start reaching out to the un-churched. Let's start having outreach programs to reach out in the community to let the community know that Mt Pleasant is in the business of saving souls!

- Remember, we come IN here to worship God. We go OUT there to serve Him!
- Let us believe on Him who died on the cross for us.
- Let us believe in one another through the power of the Holy Spirit.
- Let us be the light as Christ is the Light. God bless you!!!

It Was Prophesied in the Old Testament

The Lord's house would be established in the last days, when the law went forth from Jerusalem (Isaiah 2:2-3). Remember that the church is God's house. Nebuchadnezzar dreamed of an image (Dan. 2:31-45). It prophesied that the kingdom (church) would begin during the Roman Empire. God planned the church centuries before it began. Would the Creator and Ruler of the Universe go to such trouble for an insignificant institution? I don't think so.

Jesus Promised to Build It

Jesus promised to build His church (Matt. 16:18). People put great effort into planning something only if it is important to them. If they consider their wedding ceremony to be important, a bride and groom make many plans. Lavish neighborhoods are thought out on the drawing boards long before they are ever built. So Jesus put much effort into planning the church. Clearly it was important to Him. In particular, He came to save men from sin (Luke 19:10). While here He carefully prepared people for the church/kingdom. God's plan was a plan to save men from sin, and Jesus came to work that plan. The church then is an essential part of that plan. Therefore, the church is essential to our salvation.

Who Built <u>THIS</u> House?
Psalms 127:1

Introduction

As Christians we have our own language, don't we? We use terms/phrases that non-Christians don't understand. "Are you saved?" (*Saved from what?*) "Have you been found?" (*Found? I didn't know I was lost!*) "Have you been washed in the blood?" (*That's gross!*)

Some of the terminology we use for church can be confusing unless you are an insider. For instance when we talk about the corporate identity we might use the word kingdom or body. We understand that those terms mean our church. However, the term I want to look at is **House.**

Before I can start talking about the concept of the church as a "House", I probably need to stop and mention to you that when I use the word "house" or "church" I am not talking about this physical building. In fact, God himself tells us in *Acts 17:24* that God, even though He dwelt in a physical tabernacle in the Old Testament, no longer lives in temples built by hands. So it wouldn't matter how much stained glass, marble, or gold we adorned this building with ... God doesn't live here.

According to *1 Peter 2:5* -- **We are His house**. He brings together the discontented, the indebted, and the dismayed – those marked by pain. In His own power and ability He joins us together, fits us together, unifies us, and shapes us into a dwelling place. Our part in this is that we determine, by how we obey and respond to his shaping, whether or not we are establishing God a palace or a shack! Some of us are asking God to settle for a shack! But I believe God wants to work in us to establish and build a beautiful house for His dwelling place!

In our text we are also told that unless God builds the house the builder labors in vain. In other words, unless the house is constructed according to God's standards, God's specs, God's orders, and God's blueprint then we are wasting our time. God never lives in a house He has not built. He is not obligated to come and live in our church just because we call it a church! He will only live in what **He** builds! You can go back and discover from the Old Testament that any time the folks built something according to His plans that it was at those moments that His glory would fill the house.

I want that here, don't you? I don't want to build a clique or a club. I want to see God's house establish in and through us so that His glory will live among us! I don't want to build something and then beg God to come and bless it. He isn't obligated to do so. That is true of this house and true of your house/life. Our only hope to see His glory is to build our church/life according to His instructions.

I have discovered that in the natural every house operates differently. Each house has its own system, structure, and order. Maybe in your house the Dad was the boss. That is a **patriarchal** system.

Brothers, who built your house?

Matt 7: 26-27

And every one that heareth these sayings of mine, and doeth them not, shall be likened unto a foolish man, which built his house upon the sand: 27 And the rain descended, and the floods came, and the winds blew, and beat upon that house; and it fell: and great was the fall of it."

Jesus tells us here that the man who hears His sayings but chooses not to do them is a foolish man.

Brothers! Who built your house? When you marry the queen God has blessed you with, do you already have a house to take her to or do you expect to live with her? Who built your house?

Brothers! God has ordained **you** to be the head of your house. Are you the MAN God wants you to be in your house? You are the priest for your family. You are the provider and the protector to your wife and children so tell me Brothers, who built your house?

Brothers! Is there love in your house? Do you tell and show your wife that you love her?

Ephesians 5:25, "Husbands, love your wives, even as Christ also loved the church, and gave himself for it; ..."

Listen to these words ...

Proverbs 5:18-20, "18 Let thy fountain be blessed: and rejoice with the wife of thy youth. 19 Let her be as the loving hind and pleasant roe; let her breasts satisfy thee at all times; and be thou ravished always with her love. 20 And why wilt thou, my son, be ravished with a strange woman, and embrace the bosom of a stranger?

Brothers when you leave your wife to go into the arms of another woman you are destroying your house! Tell me Brothers, who built your house?

Remember the words of Joshua in *Josh 24:15b…"but as for me and my house, we will serve the LORD."*

Brothers! Who built your house?

Maybe in your house the order was that the Mom was the boss or the glue that held everything together. That is a **matriarchal** system.

Sisters, who built your house?

Proverbs 14:1,

"Every wise woman buildeth her house: but the foolish plucketh it down with her hands."

Sisters! Who built your house? Solomon tells us that the woman who has God to build her house is counted as being wise. Sisters! Who built your house? The Bible gives us many examples of wise women Like Ruth, Esther, and the virtuous woman of *Prov 31:10-31.*

Solomon goes on to say that the foolish woman tears down her house. Why is she called "foolish"? *Prov 9:13, "A foolish woman is clamourous: she is simple, and knoweth nothing."*

The word "clamorous" means loudmouth, yelling, screaming. The word "simple", in this context, means stupid. Therefore she is someone you don't want to be around; and the Bible says she knows nothing! Instead of having God build her house she goes to her mother, she goes to her sisters, she goes to her girlfriends! And the Bible says that except the Lord, except God builds her house it's being built in vain! Sisters! Who's built your house?

Married Sisters! Is there love in your house? ***Eph 5:22,"Wives, submit yourselves unto your own husbands, as unto the Lord."***

When you husband comes home does he come home to house of love and peace or one that's full of hate and hell? Does he have a hot meal to eat or do you tell him to fix it himself? Let me tell you something: at his job there's someone who's going to start feeding him for you. It'll be something like this: a co-worker will bring something for everybody to eat, but she'll make sure she fixes his plate. Then before you know it he's coming home full, he's already had his dinner and it wasn't from you! Sisters, who built your house?

Sisters! Are you an encourager or a deflator in your house? When was the last time you gave your husband a compliment instead of a complaint? Sisters, one of the worst things you can do to your husband and to your marriage is to criticize him in front of your children or in public. He'll start to withdraw emotionally and then you complain that he doesn't love you anymore. Sisters, who built your house?

Brothers and Sisters, husbands and wives, in ***Amos 3:3, "Can two walk together, except they be agreed?"*** What must they agree upon? The Word of God!

Jesus tells us in ***Mark 3:25, "And if a house be divided against itself, that house cannot stand."***
Single Sisters! Are you growing closer to God while your future husband is looking for you or are you going against the word of God and

you're out looking for him? ***Prov 18: 22*** says that "HE" that finds a wife finds a good thing! Notice it says "HE" and not "SHE"!

CHURCH MEMBERS, Who built *God's* House?
Mark 11:17

"17 And he taught, saying unto them, Is it not written, My house shall be called of all nations the house of prayer? but ye have made it a den of thieves."

Jesus quotes ***Isaiah 56:7*** showing the Pharisees that He knows the Word. He turns over the tables and drives the money changers out of the temple. Today we have churches that sell anything in the name of making money for the Lord: Cake walks, beauty walks, hat walks, shoe walks, car shows, fish fry's and on and on. Tell me, who's building this house? That's why I say that at Mt Pleasant no chicken and no fish have to die for Jesus!

One of the biggest enemies facing God's house is tradition. In ***Matthew 15*** and ***Mark 7*** Jesus condemns the Pharisees for not following the commandments of God and instead following their own traditions.

When it comes to worship and conducting the work of the Lord in His house we must do it His way! The old line of "We've always done it this way" is not to be allowed in God's house! When you find a pastor who allows tradition to supersede the Word of God you've found a man who needs to step down from leading God's people because he's not following God but man. Who built this house?

God knew that if He didn't give us explicit and precise instructions about how He wanted His house to be established that we would treat His house like our house and there would be no consistent structure or order. And since we would have tried to build it to suit us and to make us comfortable we would build in vain. So God very clearly gives us orders and directions on how to build His house and how His house should operate so that His blessing and His presence can dwell here. And in order for us to fit into and be productive in His house we need to understand the rules of the house!

Read ***Deuteronomy 28***. God's kingdom operates on commands and with every command there is a blessing and then there is also a curse if we don't cooperate and obey. God's house is established on the rule and on the principle of **authority**!

Mary understood authority. She is at the marriage ceremony and the wine runs out. She looks at the servants and tells them do what Jesus says to do, period. It isn't open for debate. He doesn't need your suggestions. Do what **He** says! Submit to **His** authority!

I think we would have wanted to argue with Him. We would have talked about the fact that water is heavy and so why don't we find a more convenient way to do this? We would want to fill the pots half full and then we would be shocked when we had no wine. Obey! Allow the principle of authority to produce a blessing in our lives! The seedbed for the miracle was response to authority!

We are commanded to give (Luke 6:38) and instead we tip and then we get mad because the window of heaven is closed and we struggle! Jesus isn't about giving for He's talking about obedience to authority! Because we think it's a suggestion we get mad when a preacher says we should give! We don't understand authority.

We are commanded to assemble together *(Heb 10:25)*. When you are out of church you should get nervous! I am not talking about a vacation. I am talking about the Sundays we miss just because. Just because I stayed up too late on Saturday night … Just because I would miss that good game on TV … Just because it is too pretty outside! And then we wonder why we are living under a curse? We don't understand authority!

We are commanded to think on pure things *(Phil 4:8)*, Godly things, holy things and we will go watch filth and then wonder why our minds aren't filled with peace! We don't understand the house rules!

We are commanded not to be yoked to unbelievers *(II Cor 6:14)* and yet not only will we date them, we will marry them, become bosom buddies with them, become soul tied to them and then wonder why our world is in turmoil and in a constant state of distress. We don't understand authority!

We are commanded to live at peace with everyone *(Rom 12:18)* and to avoid sowing discord among the brethren and yet we will talk about our brothers and sisters, hold grudges, blacklist one another and never make a move to correct it and then wonder why we aren't blessed. We don't obey the rules of the house!

We are commanded to submit to governing authorities *(I Peter 2:13)*, but we cheat on our taxes, cheat and steal time from our employers, disobey parents, bosses, teachers, and NOBODY ever obeys the pastor! Why? Because we don't know the rules of the house!

We are commanded to acknowledge God in all of our ways *(Prov 3:6)* and yet we will make major decisions without ever even consulting Him! We don't know the rules of the house!

Conclusion

God's house is to be a house of prayer, a house of worship, and a house of praise! Is there anybody here on this 142 year anniversary who can give God some praise? Who's here ready to hook up with Judah? True praise is permeated with productive power! True praise has the propensity, and the proclivity, and the possibility to be a powerful producer!

In *John 14:2-3*, Jesus tells us this: *"2 In my Father's house are many mansions: if it were not so, I would have told you. I go to prepare a place for you. 3 And if I go and prepare a place for you, I will come again, and receive you unto myself; that where I am, there ye may be also."*

I don't know who's built your house, but God built mine! Jesus died on a cross at a place called Calvary. He died so that all our sins may be forgiven. On the third day He rose and one day Jesus is going to come back for His church, He's coming back for His house. He's going to take it back to heaven to be with Him and God. There we will live in the house that God built for all eternity. Are you ready? Who built this house? The doors of the church are open. Glory to God!

The Church Was Purchased by Jesus' Blood

Jesus purchased the church with His blood *(Acts 20:28)*. He is the Savior of the body (church), because He gave Himself for it *(Eph. 5:23, 25)*. For this reason it is *His* church (Matt.16:18), belonging to Him *(1 Cor. 6:19, 20)*. Prior to Pentecost the church is spoken of as being in the future *(Matt. 16:18b)*, and after Pentecost it is spoken of as being then in existence *(Acts 2:47; 5:11; 8:1)*.

This agrees with the fact that the gospel, which saves men and obedience to which grants church membership, was first preached in its fullness on the day of Pentecost. Is it any wonder, then, that Peter later refers to the events of Pentecost as "the beginning" *(Acts 11:15)*?

Many groups teach the image of the church as the "bride of Christ" to explain the relation between Christ and the members of the Body. How important is this theme? The theme of Christ as Bridegroom of the Church was prepared for by the prophets and announced by John the Baptist. The Lord referred to himself as the "bridegroom." (John 3:29) The Apostle John speaks of the whole Church and of each of the faithful members of his Body as a bride "betrothed" to Christ the Lord so as to become but one spirit with him. The Church is the spotless bride of the spotless Lamb *(Rev. 22:17)*. *Ephesians 5:26-27* says that Christ loved the church so much, *"26 That he might sanctify and cleanse it with the washing of water by the word. 27 That he might present it to himself a glorious church, not having spot, or wrinkle, or any such thing; but that it should be holy and without blemish."*

Six Hours on the Cross
Mark 15:25, 33

Introduction

Have you ever wondered how long was Jesus crucified on the cross? Many of us have heard what I heard nearly all my life: "from the sixth till the ninth hour." However, in our text today we will discover that Jesus was on the cross longer than that and for a reason.

The THIRD Hour

Mark 25, 29-32, Luke 23:36-37

The Jews divided both the night and the day into four equal parts of three hours each. The first division of the day commenced at six o'clock in the morning, and ended at nine; the second commenced at nine and ended at twelve, etc. "The third" hour mentioned by Mark would therefore correspond with our nine o'clock in the morning.

Mark 15:29-30 (Railed on him.)

The passers-by kept blaspheming Jesus. **Wagging their heads.** They shook their heads in scornful disapproval. The logic behind their sarcasm was an argument from the greater to the lesser. If he could rebuild the Temple in three days, certainly he could easily come down from the cross.

Mark 15:31-32

The chief priests and the scribes likewise participated in the mockery, but among themselves. Their oft-repeated sarcasm concerning Christ's inability to save himself was in reality a denial that he could help anybody. If he could not deliver himself from suffering and death, how could he deliver anyone else?

The FOURTH Hour *Luke 23:39-42*

If thou be Christ? The better Greek text does not contain a condition. "You are the Messiah, aren't you? (Well, then,) save yourself and us!" The first thief was really sarcastic.

42. Lord, remember me when thou comest into thy kingdom. The tone of this request is utterly different from the cynical fling of the other brigand. This man showed amazing confidence in Jesus; for he saw him dying on a cross, and yet believed that he would come in a kingdom. Said (Gr. elegen) is in the imperfect tense, which means that the request was repeated. **43. Paradise** is an old Persian term for a park or a garden, a beauty spot. It became a name for the abode of God (cf. *2 Cor 12:4*).

The FIFTH Hour

John 19:26-27

John 19:26 [*Woman*] This appellation certainly implied no disrespect. [***Behold thy son!***] This refers to John, not to Jesus himself.

Behold, my beloved disciple shall be to you a son, and provide for you, and discharge toward you the duties of an affectionate child.

Mary was poor. It would even seem that now she had no home. Jesus, in his dying moments, filled with tender regard for his mother, secured for her an adopted son, obtained for her a home, and consoled her grief by the prospect of attention from him who was the most beloved of all the apostles.

John 19:27 [*Behold thy mother!*] One who is to be to thee as a mother. The fact that she was the mother of Jesus would secure the kindness of John, and the fact that she was now entrusted to him demanded of him affectionate regard and tender care.

[From that hour ...] John seems to have been in better circumstances than the other apostles. (*John 18:16*). Tradition says that she continued to live with him in Judea until the time of her death, which occurred about fifteen years after the death of Christ.

The SIXTH Hour

Mark 15:33

Three hours had passed; it was now noon, the sixth hour. At the hour of the sun's brightest light, darkness came over the whole land. This could not have been a total eclipse so that the whole earth was darkened. What caused the darkness is not stated. Certainly the timing of the phenomenon was supernatural. The ninth hour was 3:00 P.M.

The SEVENTH Hour

Nothing is said; Jesus no longer has "perfection" He now carries all of our sins.

The EIGHTH Hour

The weight of all the world's sins are bearing down on Jesus.

The NINTH Hour *Matt 27:46*

"And about the ninth hour Jesus cried with a loud voice, saying, Eli, Eli, lama sabachthani? that is to say, My God, my God, why hast thou forsaken me?"

- *Jesus is now completely and totally sin. He no longer feels the joy of God.*

John 19: 28-30

- *Jesus says, "I thirst" in verse 28 and in verse 29 they give Him some vinegar (sour wine).*
- *In verse 30 Jesus knows that His mission is now complete says, "It's finished."*

Luke 23: 46

"And when Jesus had cried with a loud voice, he said, Father, into thy hands I commend my spirit: and having said thus, he gave up the ghost."

Mark 15:37

"And Jesus cried with a loud voice, and gave up the ghost."

Matt 27:51-53

51 And, behold, the veil of the temple was rent in twain from the top to the bottom; and the earth did quake, and the rocks rent;
52 And the graves were opened; and many bodies of the saints which slept arose,
53 And came out of the graves after his resurrection, and went into the holy city, and appeared unto many.

- Satan and his demons begin to celebrate their "victory"
- Death has taken Jesus to the grave.
- For nearly three days and three nights the grave has Jesus.

However after the third night the grave calls Satan telling him that there's a problem. Jesus is moving again and He's getting up out of the grave! Satan yells at the grave to hold Him but the grave says this man is alive once again! Satan orders death to kill Jesus one more time. But death tells Satan "I can't kill Him again because the Scripture says, **'And as it is appointed unto men once to die'** so you better do something else."

But no matter what Satan tried to do, Jesus, our Blessed Hope, Jesus, my Redeemer, Jesus, my Lord and Savior, got up He rose from the grave victorious over the death and the grave. He lives! He lives! Thank God almighty Jesus Christ lives!!!

Jesus is alive and well. The Bible tells us that He sits right now on the right hand of God the Father. One day, when God tells Him to come back for His church, He will. He's coming back! He's coming back!! HE"S COMING BACK!!! Will you be ready? I'm ready right now! Are YOU? Come to Jesus while you still have time. The doors to the church are open. Glory to GOD!

The love of Christ was so strong that He purchased the church with His own blood. In *1 Corinthian 6:19-20* Paul reminds us saying, *"19 What? know ye not that your body is the temple of the Holy Ghost which is in you, which ye have of God, and ye are not your own? 20 For ye are bought with a price: therefore glorify God in your body, and in your spirit, which are God's."*

The "price" that Paul refers to was the very life of Jesus when He died on the cross at Calvary and *"gave himself for it (Eph. 5:25)"*. When Christ rose after three days and three nights the purchase was complete. The church is now purified. The bride is now ready to receive the bridegroom. Let's now observe the first church and how it began in Chapter Three.

Chapter Three

The First Church

The first local church met in Jerusalem. Its membership was made up of ordinary people: fishermen, farmers, and poor people. However, the congregation was also made up of people who were well off as indicated by their sharing of their goods so that all were equal according to their needs *(Acts 2:45)*. This first church was born during a prayer meeting on the Day of Pentecost. The Holy Spirit arrived and filled those who were waiting for Him in the upper room. It should also be noted that those in the upper room were gathered on one accord. This is to say that they were in harmony and peace with one another. They were filled by the Spirit and experienced the manifestation of the unity of Spirit and the love of Christ. This outpouring led to the rapid growth of the church. As recorded in *Acts 2: 41* three thousand souls were added that very day.[4]

How they Worshiped

Throughout most centuries of Church history, Christian worship has been primarily liturgical, characterized by prayers and hymns, whose texts were rooted in, or closely related to, the Scripture, and particularly the Psalter. Set times for prayer during the day were established and a festal cycle throughout the Church year governed the celebration of feasts and holy days pertaining to the events in the life of Jesus, the lives of the saints, and aspects of the Church's perception of God.

In his *First Apology*, a letter of defense written to Roman emperor, Antonius Pius, 161-180, Justin described simple Christian worship services and practices, explaining:

- "...after we have thus washed him who has been convinced (converted to Christianity) and has assented to our teaching, we bring him to the place where those who are called brethren are assembled, in order that we may offer hearty prayers in common for ourselves and for the baptized person, ...so that we may be saved with an everlasting salvation. Having ended the prayers, we salute one another with a kiss. There is then brought to the president of the brethren bread and a cup of wine mixed with water; and he taking them, gives praise and glory to the Father of the universe, through the name of the Son and of the Holy Ghost, and offers thanks at considerable length for our being counted worthy to receive these things at His hands. And when he has concluded the prayers and thanksgivings, all the people present express their assent by saying 'Amen'".
- When the president has given thanks, and all the people have expressed their assent, those who are called by us deacons give to each of those present to partake of the bread and wine mixed with water over which the thanksgiving was pronounced, and to those who are absent they carry away a portion....And this food is called among us Eucharistia or (the Eucharist), of which no one is

allowed to partake but the man who believes that the things which we teach are true, and who has been washed with the washing that is for the remission of sins, and unto regeneration, and who is so living as Christ has enjoined. ... we, being taught that the food which is blessed by the prayer of His word, and from which our blood and flesh by transmutation are nourished, is the flesh and blood of that Jesus who was made flesh. For the apostles, in the memoirs composed by them, which are called Gospels, have thus delivered unto us what was enjoined upon them; that Jesus took bread, and when He had given thanks, said, **"This do ye in remembrance of Me, this is My body;"** and that, after the same manner, having taken the cup and given thanks, He said, **"This is My blood;" and gave it to them alone."** [5]

Worship included Songs

The very early development of Christian worship is lost in the mists of history, but Christian worship is, in general, rooted in the worship of Judaism of the Second Temple period. The Gospels and the Acts of the Apostles present the very early Christians, then still very much a part of the Jewish scene, as frequenting both the Temple and synagogues, as well as worshipping in private homes, frequently to "break bread," a term which connotes both the sharing of a meal and, within that context, celebrating the Eucharist. *Acts 2:42* presents the very early Church of Jerusalem as "continuing in the Apostles' teaching and fellowship (or "communion), the breaking of bread, and the prayers."

Psalms and hymns based on them were a regular feature of Jewish worship in the synagogues, and these were also incorporated into Christian hymns. The Psalms are still frequently quoted and paraphrased in nearly all the different Christian traditions and denominations.

The gospels of *Matthew (26:30)* and *Mark (14:26)* state that Jesus sang a hymn with his disciples immediately before his betrayal. The apostle Paul in the book of *Ephesians (5:19)* exhorted the church at Ephesus to speak to each other "in psalms and hymns and spiritual songs, singing and making melody in your heart to the Lord". In the book of *Colossians (3:16)* he also encouraged the church at Colossae to teach and admonish each other with "psalms and hymns and spiritual songs".

The Purpose for the Church
I Samuel 21:1-9

Introduction

What is the purpose for the church? Is it a place where we come to worship God? Is it a building that we proudly show our visitors and friends? Is it a place where we come to hear from heaven? Just what do YOU come to church for?

"And this is his commandment, That we should believe on the name of his Son Jesus Christ, and love one another, as he gave us commandment."

Luke 14:23, "And the lord said unto the servant, Go out into the highways and hedges, and compel them to come in, that my house may be filled."

If we want the church to grow we must go out and find them! If we sit in here and wait for the lost, the un-churched, to come, we'll still be here waiting on Jesus. Jesus tells us to go out and find them! So, let's start reaching out to the un-churched. Let's start having outreach programs to reach out in the community to let the community know that Mt Pleasant is in the business of saving souls!

Remember, we come IN here to worship God. We go OUT there to serve Him!

Let us believe on Him who died on the cross for us. Let us believe in one another through the power of the Holy Spirit. Let us be the light as Christ is the Light. God bless you!!!

The Church's Ministry

The mission of the church was simple: Teach sound doctrine. In *Titus 2:1 Paul* says, *"But speak thou the things which become sound doctrine."*

This was accomplished by an evangelist who would go into an area where there were no Christians, win some people ever to Christ by preaching the gospel and establish a congregation. The evangelist would stay there for as long as a year, if necessary, assisting the new church. Once members matured in the Word of God the evangelist would appoint elders in that city to care for and feed the new church. The evangelist would then move on to another place and start the process over again.

The concept of starting churches is a paramount movement because the process of forming Godly disciples is necessarily social. "Church" should be understood in the widest sense, as an organization of believers. It is not a building. Many churches start by meeting in houses. The making of disciples is required to grow the number of believers to the largest extent, maximize their quality, and therefore making their worship acceptable to God.

The Spread of Christianity

As we know, Christianity began as an offshoot of Judaism - Jesus was a Jew, as were all the disciples and most of the first converts, and Jesus fulfilled Judaic hopes of a Messiah. The Church stayed centered at Jerusalem (map: J10) initially, with missionaries going out to the surrounding districts. After the fall of Jerusalem in 70 AD, the home of the Church moved to Antioch of Syria (J8).

It soon became apparent that the easiest converts in those early times were Gentile Jews - i.e., those who weren't Jewish by birth yet believed the Jewish Testament (this may be because the evangelists could have preached a message along the lines of: "You can have all that Judaism has to offer and more, and you do not have to be circumcised!" - circumcision was looked down upon by Romans and Greeks). There is evidence that a Church in India was established very early on; it is in fact held by some that the Apostle Thomas started that church.

The central Church soon moved to Rome (E6), and once it settled in, became very influential (this would be expected, as Rome was a very large city). Information on exact movements is unreliable, but it is clear that by the middle of the Second Century, a significant body of believers existed in Gaul (France, C4), obviously others scattered around the Mediterranean; and by end of the Third Century AD in Spain (A6), Britain (C1), North Africa (D8), Cyrene (G10), and Alexandria (I10) (the last of which claims John Mark as their founder).

In short, by the time of the first Christian Roman Emperor (Constantine in 312), no area of the Roman Empire was left without a Christian witness; with the strongest areas of Christian influence being in Syria (J8), North Africa (D8), Asia Minor, Egypt (I12), Rome (E6) and Lyons (D4). It does seem, however, that those who lived in small villages were untouched by the spread of Christianity.[6]

It must be a movement because special organization is required for the task of planting churches. This movement naturally forms cross-cultural missions, when persons who understand and accept church-planting duties go to people outside their culture, as Christ commanded in the Great Commission *(Matt. 28:18-20)*. Thus the cycle repeats. For example, a missionary goes into a foreign country where the Gospel of Jesus Christ has never been taught. Sometimes missionaries go in teams or as families. The missionary is provided for by his (her) home church as he ministers the Word of God to the native people. Several hurdles must be crossed with language being one of the largest. As the number of people are converted the necessity for a church (building) becomes paramount. This is the pinnacle of the missionary effort for as the sanctuary is built in the physical, it has already been established in the spiritual.

This concludes Part I. In Part II we will take a close look at the church of today and see if it is still the same or if it has changed.

Part II

The Present

The Church of Today

Chapter Four

What happened to the Church?

When one looks back at the first church with all its history and then looks at the church of today, one must ask the question, "What happened?" The church of today pales significantly to the church of yesterday.

Spiritual Amnesia

Romans 13:11

Introduction

If I were to ask you who are you, you would tell me your name. But what if you didn't know your name? What if you suddenly could not remember were you lived? That would be a scary situation wouldn't it? When you cannot remember anything you are said to be suffering from amnesia. **Amnesia** is defined as a temporary loss of memory that can be caused by injury, disease, or alcoholism. Today more than ever there are too many Christians suffering from spiritual amnesia, forgetting who they are in the body of Christ. It is my prayer that after hearing this message you will not develop spiritual amnesia and how to help those who have. Today we're going to look at spiritual amnesia by first reviewing who we are, then look at some causes of spiritual amnesia, and finally the cure.

Born Again

When we are born again we take on a new identity. While we make look the same on the outside we are a new person on the inside. Turn to **Romans 8:14**. There the Bible tells us that as we *"are led by the Spirit of God, we are the sons of God."* Now, in *versus 15* we are told that we have not received the spirit of bondage, *"**But you have received the Spirit of adoption**.* A sanctified soul bears the image of God, as the child bears the image of the father. *"Whereby we cry, Abba, Father"* and we have received the Spirit of the Son:

- *"To witness to the relation of children," versus 16.* The former is the work of the Spirit as a Sanctifier; this as a Comforter. *"If children, then heirs", versus 17.*
- In earthly inheritances this rule does not hold, only the first-born are heirs; but the church is a church of first-born, for they are all heirs. Heaven is an inheritance that all the saints are heirs to **Heirs of God.** The Lord himself is the portion of the saints' inheritance.
- **Joint-heirs with Christ**. Christ, as Mediator, is said to be the heir of all things (**Hebrew 1:2**), and true believers, by virtue of their union with him, shall inherit all things, **Rev 21:7**. Those that now partake of the Spirit of Christ, as his brethren, shall, as his

brethren, partake of his glory (***John 17:24***), shall sit down with him upon his throne, ***Rev 3:21***.

Causes of Spiritual Amnesia

Now that we have a better understanding of who we are in the body of Christ, what could cause us to forget this wonderful revelation? What could cause us to fall asleep as mentioned in our text? Let's see?

Grief

When we suffer the loss of a loved one, we often develop spiritual amnesia. You see Death has a way of causing us to forget everything we know about God. We question Him and His will. Sometimes we get so carried away that we start to think like Job's wife and want to simply curse God and die. We turn to alcohol, drugs, anything to cause us to "forget" the pain we are suffering. But the most important things we forget can be found in ***Hebrew 13:5*** where Jesus says," I'll never leave thee, nor forsake thee." He will never give us more than we are able to bear.

Loss of a job

Some of us forget who God is when we lose our jobs. We forget that all the money in earth belongs to God. We forget that the cattle on a thousand hills belong to Him. We forget ***Philippians 4:19, "But my God shall supply all your need according to his riches in glory by Christ Jesus."*** We develop spiritual amnesia.

Backsliding

When we stop going to church, stop attending Sunday school, stop going to Bible Study, we start to forget about being faithful to God. The ways of the world begins to resurrect the old man that died when we were born again. Slowly, day by day, we forget all about our soul salvation. We forget the Bible says that we cannot serve two masters. For example, you cannot study read your Bible with the radio or TV on. You cannot study your Sunday school lesson and try to watch a movie at the same time. And as proof that we are losing our minds we claim that we can do both at the same time. But we forgot in **Luke 16:13 Jesus** said,

"No servant can serve two masters: for either he will hate the one, and love the other; or else he will hold to the one, and despise the other. Ye cannot serve God and mammon.

And in **Proverbs 28:9** it says

"He that turneth away his ear from hearing the law, even his prayer shall be abomination."

Now we sleep in late on Sunday mornings instead of going to Sunday school. Now we wash and wax our cars on Sunday instead of attending morning worship service. Now we go to Bingo on Wednesday nights instead of going to Bible Study. Now we have spiritual amnesia.

I must say, however, that spiritual amnesia does not limit itself to just the congregation. My fellow preachers, do you know who you are? You see, for too long we have not been aware of whom we truly are. The reason I say that is when you hand me your business card, when I look at your church bulletin, your church van, or your church marquee, I see the same thing. Rev So and So, Pastor So and So. What's wrong with that? Turn to *Eph 4:11*. Let's read this verse slowly and carefully.

The first thing to understand is that these are the spiritual gifts that were given by Christ. Let's begin. Some apostles some prophets and some Evangelists, some Pastors and Teachers.

How many "somes" did you count? Four! Look at the word "and". This word is a conjunction. It is used to hook up or connect two things together to make one. Pastor and teachers go together. We need to remember that Jesus did more teaching than preaching. Often He was called "Rabbi" which is the Jewish word for "teacher." Jesus would **preach** to the crowds, but He always **taught** His disciples.

In Luke 11:1 one of the disciples asks Him to teach them how to pray. From this request we have the Lord's Prayer. My fellow pastors, are you also teaching? If so, then be sure to include it on your business card and so forth. Now, if you're not teaching your congregation who is? The Bible says in *Hos 4:6*

"My people are destroyed for lack of knowledge: because thou hast rejected knowledge, I will also reject thee, that thou shalt be no priest to me: seeing thou hast forgotten the law of thy God, I will also forget thy children."

The Cure

Romans 13:11

The cure for spiritual amnesia is simple. In *versus 11b* and *11c,* we are told that now is the time to wake up! Go to Sunday school, go to church, attend Bible Study weekly. Take a daily dose of Bible reading and studying.

Finally pray at least five times daily (first thing in the morning, once at meal times, and before going to sleep at night). Doing these things will insure that you will always know who you are in the body of Christ, and that your chances of getting spiritual amnesia will all but disappear.

The cure also involves all of us looking out for our fellow brothers and sisters in Christ. Remember, spiritual amnesia can happen to anyone. We are reminded to that those of us who are strong are to bear the infirmities of the weak. Our salvation is closer now more than ever.

Conclusion

Today we have looked at spiritual amnesia. We were reminded of who we are in the body of Christ. We looked at some things that can cause spiritual amnesia. Spiritual amnesia is not limited to just the congregation; preachers can also develop it.

The Pastor

The pastor is literally, a helper or feeder of the sheep. Besides the literal sense the word now has a figurative meaning: it refers to the minister appointed over a congregation. In New Testament times the pastor was the feeder, protector, and guide, or shepherd of a flock of God's people.

In speaking of spiritual gifts, the apostle Paul wrote that **Christ "gave some to be apostles, some prophets, some evangelists, and some pastors and teachers" (Eph 4:11).** The term "Pastor" by this time in church history had not yet become an official title. The term implied the nourishing of and caring of God's people.

Armed with this definition, we can now look at the pastor of today's church. Sadly, instead of seeing a man of God who is doing the will of God, we more than often discover a *professional*. True pastors are **not** professionals! Pastors are fools for the sake of Christ (*I Cor. 4:10*) where professionals are wise to the world and not to Christ.

Paul says that the pastor can pass for fools in the world and even be despised as such. However, faithful pastors can bear being despised, so that the wisdom of God and the power of His grace are thereby displayed. True pastors are most emphatically not part of a social team sharing goals with other professionals. The goal of a pastor is to preach Jesus Christ crucified; to the professional (Greek) this is foolishness (as Paul says in *1 Cor. 1:23*). When a pastor loses his focus on his true calling, he becomes a professional.

The world sets the agenda of the professional man; God sets the agenda of the spiritual man. The pastor who becomes a professional is more concerned with the attendance than with the attitude. He's more concerned with the amount raised in the collection plate than the number of saved souls. The strong wine of Jesus Christ explodes the wineskins of professionalism. There is an infinite difference between the pastor whose heart is set on being a professional and the pastor whose heart is set on being the aroma of Christ, the fragrance of death to some and life eternal to others (*2 Cor. 2:15-16*).[7]

The Work of a Pastor

Nehemiah 6:1-19

Introduction

The work of a pastor is task that has no time clock. While he is a pastor the man of God is on call 24 hours a day, 7 days a week. During the course of this position there are many programs and projects that are started, yet many are not finished. One reason for this is that we can be distracted from the task of doing the Lord's work. It's so easy to get sidetracked isn't it? It takes tenacity to finish what we start because there are always so many competing distractions.

One thing that clearly emerges from our study in the Book of Nehemiah is that life is a battle from beginning to end. In *Ephesians 6:12* the Apostle Paul warns;

"For we wrestle not against flesh and blood, but against principalities, against powers, against the rulers of the darkness of this world, against spiritual wickedness in high places."

In our text, we meet those powers and rulers of the darkness of this world. ***Nehemiah 6***, as in many other places in Scripture, we learn that the devil has two main ways of working. The first tactic is fear. Satan is prowling around, as Peter says in ***1 Peter 5:8***, *"like a roaring lion looking for someone to devour."*

But he has another battle plan as well. He not only uses fear, he also utilizes flattery.

II Corinthians 11:14 reveals that Satan *"masquerades as an angel of light."*

He comes with enticing promises and flattering words, assuring us that what he proposes will cost us nothing. Whatever method the evil one employs, whether it is fear or flattery, his aim is to distract and destroy us. We need to be on guard against each of these approaches. That is why Paul says in ***II Corinthians 2:11*** that *"We are not unaware of his schemes."* We need to be on guard because Satan is both a lion that devours and a serpent that deceives.

When you do the work of the Lord, the enemy will try to distract you. If he can distract you he can discourage you. If he can discourage you he can destroy you.

The Lure

Nehemiah 6:1-4

Since Sanballat and his sinister buddies failed in their attempts to stop the wall builders, they decide to concentrate their attacks on Nehemiah himself by changing their tactics and resorting to subtle persuasion. We might call this political softball. You will experience this as well when you try to correct some things in your life. Many people today are faltering in their Christian pilgrimage because they listen to the advice and temptations of those closest to them.

Let's take a look at **Nehemiah 6:1-4:** *"Now it came to pass when Sanballat, and Tobiah, and Geshem the Arabian, and the rest of our enemies, heard that I had built the wall, and that there was no breach left therein; (though at that time I had not set up the doors upon the gates;*

That Sanballat and Geshem sent unto me, saying, Come, let us meet together in some one of the villages in the plain of Ono. But they thought to do me mischief.

And I sent messengers unto them, saying, I am doing a great work, so that I cannot come down: why should the work cease, whilst I leave it, and come down to you?

Yet they sent unto me four times after this sort; and I answered them after the same manner."

These enemies suddenly become Nehemiah's friends and invite him to a conference down on the plain of Ono. The first four verses look like a political concession speech they want to meet with Nehemiah and cut their losses or so it seems. Ono is located on the seacoast near the Gaza strip. It was a beautiful resort area. But Nehemiah senses danger: *"they were scheming to harm me."* So Nehemiah said, "Oh, no!" to Ono.

Some commentators suggest that they were trying to trick him into leaving Jerusalem, where he had armed support, to come to a conference where they could ambush him. Nehemiah evidently senses this. He firmly declines, saying, "I am carrying on a great project, and I cannot go down. Why should the work stop while I leave it and go down to you?"

That is a great answer even though it sounds rather blunt. But Nehemiah sees through their scheme by refusing their invitation four different times. You, too, may experience continuing pressure to change your mind and go along with something that is wrong. Some of us give in to repeated pressure. We might decline the first invitation but find our defenses weakened as the enticements continue. But Nehemiah persists in his refusal because he knows what his priorities are: "I am doing a great work. I have a great calling. God has committed a tremendous project to me, and if I leave, it will be threatened."

One of the most helpful things that we can do to resist temptation is to remember that God has called each of us to a great task. This is true of every believer in Christ whether you're just become a Christian today or you've been here for many years. We are called to make a kingdom impact. Our priorities as a church should be to make an impact to the world for Christ.

Friends, in a similar way, we've been called to a great task one that we have to prioritize or we'll be distracted from it. If we don't practice some "planned neglect" of other things, even good things, we'll be distracted from God's best. That's what Nehemiah does. He's involved in a great work, and he's not going to forsake it for anything less.

The Letter

Nehemiah 6:5-9

When the enemy cannot accomplish his purpose by offering peace, he switches back to his original scheme of sinister threats. He moves from political softball to political hardball.
Take a look *at verses 5 - 7*

"Then sent Sanballat his servant unto me in like manner the fifth time with an open letter in his hand

Wherein was written, It is reported among the heathen, and Gashmu saith it, that thou and the Jews think to rebel: for which cause thou buildest the wall, that thou mayest be their king, according to these words.

And thou hast also appointed prophets to preach of thee at Jerusalem, saying, There is a king in Judah: and now shall it be reported to the king according to these words. Come now therefore, and let us take counsel together."

This arm-twisting tactic is designed to pressure Nehemiah to yield to their request, and thus fall into their trap. But he resists because he sees it for what it really is, an enticement based upon lies. Note that it was an "unsealed letter." In other words, it was designed for everyone to read, so that the lie would be spread around that Nehemiah was trying to make himself king.

Have you ever noticed that rumors regularly cite people of distinction as sources? That's what happened here *"and Geshem says it's true."* Someone has said that gossip is news you have to hurry to tell somebody else before you find out it isn't true!

Nehemiah responded three different ways he denied the rumor, he prayed to God for strength, and he went back to work.

Look at *verse 8: "Then I sent unto him, saying, There are no such things done as thou sayest, but thou feignest them out of thine own heart."*

And then, invariably, as was his practice, he responds with another "popcorn prayer" in *verse 9:*

"For they all made us afraid, saying, Their hands shall be weakened from the work, that it be not done. Now therefore, O God, strengthen my hands."

Their tactics were to get the people to think that Nehemiah had some hidden motive -- his own glory -- for rebuilding the wall, hoping that the workers would thus become discouraged and quit. Nehemiah simply prays, "Lord, do not let that happen. Strengthen me to work all the harder." They were on the last lap of the race and the finish line was in sight. He took care of his character and trusted God to take care of his reputation.

The Lie

Nehemiah 6:10-15

Once again the enemy switches his game plan in **verse 10:** *Afterward I came unto the house of Shemaiah the son of Delaiah the son of Mehetabeel, who was shut up; and he said, Let us meet together in the house of God, within the temple, and let us shut the doors of the temple: for they will come to slay thee; yea, in the night will they come to slay thee.*

This false prophet claims to have hidden knowledge. That is suggested by the phrase, *"he was shut in"* at his home. He was secluding himself for some religious reason. This is frequently the case with those who claim to be psychics who are in touch with the invisible world. They sit behind curtains in semi-darkness, trying to create a sense of mystery, as though they know more about inscrutable things than others.

What he says sounds logical: "Some people are out to get you. They are going to kill you." Nehemiah certainly believes that! The man suggests, "Come on up here and we will go into the temple and shut the doors. They will not dare attack you there." That sounds good, but immediately Nehemiah detects that something is wrong. He knows that he is not permitted to go into the temple, for only priests could enter the holy place.

So he answers in *verse 11: "And I said, Should such a man as I flee? and who is there, that, being as I am, would go into the temple to save his life? I will not go in."*

Having right priorities gave Nehemiah the courage to do what was right. Courage isn't the absence of fear but instead it's the tenacity to do what is right no matter how much we're afraid. You see, it's not just a matter of saying 'no' to distractions. We have to first say 'yes' to the right things, so that our priorities match up with God's priorities. As we keep the main thing the main thing, we'll be able to deal with distractions the way Nehemiah did.

God gives Nehemiah some insight in *verses 12-13, " And, lo, I perceived that God had not sent him; but that he pronounced this prophecy against me: for Tobiah and Sanballat had hired him.*

Therefore was he hired, that I should be afraid, and do so, and sin, and that they might have matter for an evil report, that they might reproach me."

It was all part of a plan to discourage and distract the people from following Nehemiah's lead. Fueled by jealousy and ambition, these enemies slandered him and tried to trick him into yielding to their demands.

We must be aware of this kind of attack in our lives as well. Don't take someone's advice or do what a friend asks you to do just because they seem like a nice person. Don't let anyone or anything distract you from God's priorities. The best response to such an approach is what Nehemiah uses here -- a deep sense of his true identity as a believer. "Should a man like me run and hide and try to save his life by wrong approaches and unlawful practices?" He falls back upon his clear understanding of who he is and what his priorities are. He is a believer in the Living God and as such need not resort to trickery to save his life.

Nehemiah meets this attack of the enemy by going to prayer once again in ***verse 14. " My God, think thou upon Tobiah and Sanballat according to these their works, and on the prophetess Noadiah, and the rest of the prophets, that would have put me in fear."***

Brothers and sisters, here's one of the overriding truths from this book: the devil never quits. He is never going to give up while we are still alive. God has wonderful blessings and much encouragement and joy for us along the way, but we must never cease battling against the world, the flesh and the devil until we get to heaven. The enemy of God will never quit. If he cannot distract you with fear and flattery, he will use gossip and false accusations.

But if have on the whole Armour of God, you will be able to stand. Stand on the solid rock of your faith…stand on the Jesus, the Word of God! God bless you!

The Congregation

There are many things that can hurt a church and destroy its testimony. The primary one is poor leadership or false teachers (prophets) who fail to build the church on the Word of God.

The second cause follows the first: a church where the congregation doesn't follow its leadership. This causes church splits as well as other problems that are exposed to the full view of the world.

Every church member must follow the design of the Spirit and be faithful and obedient.

The congregation is the part of the church that is to do *"the work of the ministry" (Eph. 4:12).* The role of the congregation is further explained in *Hebrew13:17, "Obey them that have the rule over you, and submit yourselves: for they watch for your souls, as they that must give account, that they may do it with joy, and not with grief: for that is unprofitable for you."*

The church as presented in our culture is represented as, "that church building on the corner", or "that Christian denomination." The state of Mississippi, my home state, has more churches per capita, than any other state in the United States. Why so many churches? One reason may be due to the congregations' inability to follow its leadership. Therefore, when one mentions the word "Church" one must remember that there are two distinct definitions:

- The first is spiritual: made up exclusively of leaders and members who are true believers in Jesus Christ. This is a true church.
- The second is secular: local, national and international organizations with believing and unbelieving leaders and members.

Ask the question, "What's wrong with the church organizations that call themselves Christian?" Just take a look at these church organizations and you'll have your answer. They are having more pastors being exposed today for sinful practices than ever. The lavish lifestyles that many of these pastors live, compared to the congregation they are supposed to minister to, is outlandish. Churches that are harming instead of healing are on the rise. Is it no wonder that many are leaving these so-called churches?

On the other hand, if the question was, "What's wrong with the Church today?" The answer would be nothing. For Jesus said, ***"You are the salt of the earth." ... "You are the light of the world" (Matt. 5:13-14).***[8]

The People Who come to Church
Matthew 13:24-30

Introduction

In today's text Jesus is talking about the presence of good and evil in this world. Jesus tells them this: *"The kingdom of heaven is like a man who sowed good seed in his field. But while everyone was sleeping, his enemy came and sowed weeds among the wheat, and went away. When the wheat sprouted and formed heads, then the weeds also appeared.*

"The owner's servants came to him and said, 'Sir, didn't you sow good seed in your field? Where then did the weeds come from?' 'An enemy did this,' he replied. The servants asked him, 'Do you want us to go and pull them up?'' 'No,' he answered, 'because while you are pulling the weeds, you may root up the wheat with them. Let both grow together until the harvest. At that time I will tell the harvesters: First collect the weeds and tie them in bundles to be burned; then gather the wheat and bring it into my barn.'"

In this parable Jesus says that as wheat and weeds grow side by side they look a lot alike. And if we were to try to pull up the weeds we would likely uproot the wheat as well. So we are told to let them grow until the harvest. Then it will be easy to see which is which, and to treat them accordingly.

Jesus told this parable nearly 2,000 years ago. But the lessons He was teaching are just as applicable today. So let's consider some of them.

Reality of Hypocrisy

- The first one is the reality of hypocrisy. Jesus says that there will be both good and evil people in this world, and they'll be living side by side.

Even the church will not be immune to this mixture. On the one hand, it seems unfair to say that the church is full of hypocrites, because I know a lot of people who have been faithful and true and authentic in their Christian lives, and they're wonderful Christian people. But even those of us who have been Christians for many years have experienced times when our guard was down and Satan shot his fiery darts, and sin was the result.

- Now there is a difference between a Christian struggling with sin and a hypocrite. If you're struggling with a sin, you come to God saying, "God, this is a weakness in my life and I really need the help of the Holy Spirit to deal with it."

God welcomes that prayer and He promises to help. But the hypocrite doesn't really struggle to overcome his sin. He just tries to hide it. He thinks, "When I'm in church I'll behave like a Christian. I'll say the prayers. I'll sing the songs. I'll obey the rules. But when I'm out in the world I become a different person who behaves exactly the way the world behaves."

The word "hypocrite" originally came from a word used in Greek drama that meant "one who is play-acting, wearing a mask." The symbol of Greek drama, as you may know, is a two-faced mask. That's why a hypocrite is often called "two-faced," someone who is trying to deceive, pretending to be better than he or she really is.

A preacher in the Midwest tells about a young couple in his church who boasted to all their friends & neighbors that they were flying to New York City. They were only going to be able to spend one day there, but the highlight of their trip would be to go and see the Broadway play, "My Fair Lady." They were so proud of this, and everyone was really impressed because no one else in that small town had ever been to a play on Broadway.

The day came, and when they arrived in New York they took a taxi to the theatre where "My Fair Lady" was playing. To their dismay, they found that the play was sold out for the night.

They thought, "What do we do now? Everybody knows that we came to see 'My Fair Lady.' We don't dare tell them that we didn't." So they found a couple of ticket stubs on the sidewalk & picked them up. They bought a program that described the various acts of the play. They went home singing "I Could Have Danced all Night." And they told everybody that they had gone to see "My Fair Lady."

The preacher said, "That's right. They had the ticket stubs. They had the program. They had been to the theatre. They knew the music. But the trouble is they didn't see the performance." Then he added, "A lot of Christians are like that. We come to church. We have the bulletin.

We know the songs. We know what to say and what to do. The problem is that many of us have never really made Jesus the Lord of our lives."

- It's exhausting to live a two-faced life, pretending to be what you aren't, acting one way around Christians and just the opposite around others.

To have to pretend constantly that you are someone you aren't just drains you of your energy. That's why many social events are so exhausting. You go to a party and you try to pretend that you're having a good time. When, in reality, you would rather be home watching a movie on TV. But there you are - pretending. And you go home exhausted.

That's why coming to church can sometimes be an exhausting experience. If you're play-acting, pretending to be someone that you're not, you'll leave here wrung out, because you have spent more than an hour of your life pretending to be something that you aren't.

- It's not only exhausting, it's also repulsive.

One of the questions that were asked a lot last year as the government went through a time of turmoil was, "Can someone be one thing in his private life and another in his public life?"

Now that's a legitimate question. Nathaniel Hawthorne answered it a long time ago. He said, "No man, for any considerable period, can wear one face to himself and another to the multitudes without finally getting bewildered as to which is the true one." You can get so confused that you're not sure who you are anymore.

Jesus condemned hypocrisy. Listen to His words in **Matthew 23:17-28.** *"Woe to you, teachers of the law and Pharisees, you* *hypocrites! You are like whitewashed tombs; which look beautiful on the outside but on the inside are full of dead men's bones and everything unclean. In the same way, on the outside you appear to people as righteous but on the inside you are full of hypocrisy and wickedness."*

The story is told about a little boy who found a rat in his back yard. He jumped on it. He stomped on it. And he killed it. He was so proud of himself, and he ran to show it to his mother. But he didn't realize that the preacher had come to call. So the excited boy ran into the house, carrying the rat by the tail, hollering to his mom, "Mom, look what I found. I found this rat. I jumped on it, I stomped on it, and..." Just then he noticed the preacher and he finished his sentence by saying, "And then the Lord called him home."

It's terrible to have to remember to change in keeping with the company that you keep. And that's hypocrisy.

The Refusal to Judge

Here is a lesson we must learn – and it has to do with judging. In His parable, when the servants came and asked, "Do you want us to go out and pull them up?" The answer was "No, because while you're pulling up the weeds you may uproot the wheat with them. So let both grow together until harvest, and at that time I'll tell the harvesters, "First collect the weeds and tie them in bundles to be burned; then gather the wheat to bring into my barn."

In other words, Jesus is saying, "Your job is not to judge the hypocrites. I've never commissioned you to do that. So don't go into the church and start uprooting the hypocrites."

- First of all, that we're not to judge a person's salvation. That's not our job. God never put us on the judgment throne to say this person is lost and this one is saved. My responsibility is to do my best to present the truth that's in God's Word, and to leave the rest in God's hands.
- Secondly, we're not to judge another person's motives. We don't know the circumstances and why they do what they do. We don't know their background, their emotions, or what's going on inside of them. God knows, so leave that in God's hands!
- There are things, however, that we should judge. The Bible very clearly teaches that we are to recognize and judge false teachings.

Jesus says in *Matthew 7:15 "Watch out for false prophets. They come to you in sheep's clothing, but inwardly they are ferocious wolves. By their fruit you will recognize them."*

Do you see the parallels between these words and the parable we've been reading? Jesus says that false teachers may look like sheep, and sound like sheep, and act like sheep. So how will we recognize them? Jesus says, "By their fruit you will recognize them." If they're sowing seeds of discord & bitterness; if they're causing people to become disobedient, then they're false teachers. **We are to judge false teaching.**

We're to judge sinful actions. If someone in the church is doing a sinful thing and its common knowledge among the brethren, then the church needs to act.

Paul uses an example in *1 Corinthians 5* of a man who was sleeping with his father's wife, and the church knew about it. So Paul condemned the church because it didn't take any action. Now what kind of action should it have taken? Paul said, "You should have gone to him to seek a reconciliation that would cause him to repent of his sin and change his ways." And if the man refused to repent, then they should expel him from among them, in the hope that he would come to his senses and repent.

But if someone who isn't a Christian comes to the church seeking Christ, they can come regardless of their sin. That's what the church is for. No matter what your past has been, if you are here genuinely seeking a relationship with the Lord, you are welcome here. But once you become a Christian. Once you have been forgiven, that changes the standards. Then if you slip back into sin, reconciliation and repentance need to take place.

Paul said, "I prayed that they should repent and turn to God and prove their repentance by their deeds."

There are reasons for Integrity

"Why should we be genuine & true?" Why should we want to be an authentic person and not a hypocrite? Because we will be respected.

The Bible says, ***"The righteous will shine like the sun in the kingdom of their father." Matthew 13:43a***

Back in the early 1950's there were three young men who were rising to the top as far as evangelists were concerned in the evangelical circles of Christendom. All three were doing well, but two of them were especially outstanding. And everybody anticipated that these two would be the greatest evangelists, perhaps, that our country had ever seen. But both of them soon dropped by the wayside. One became addicted to drugs and alcohol and the other one took his own life.

But the third one, the one who seemed the least promising at the time, remained steadfast and true. And God has used him in tremendous ways. Some have tried their best to find anything that would show him to be less than genuine in his commitment to Christ. But they have failed. And such is the respect that he has earned that in North Carolina. There is a Freeway that the state has named after him.

Today, Billy Graham's witness for Christ and the respect he has earned is stronger than it has ever been, all because he was genuine, steadfast, and true.

Edgar Guest wrote, "I'd rather see a sermon than hear one any day, I'd rather one would walk with me than merely tell the way; The eye's a better pupil and more willing than the ear, fine counsel is confusing, but examples are always clear." I may not understand the high advice you give, but there's no misunderstanding how you act and how you live.

Conclusion

A long time ago, the apostle Paul wrote, ***"Therefore God exalted him to the highest place and gave him the name that is above every name, that at the name of Jesus every knee should bow, in heaven and on earth and under the earth, and every tongue confess that Jesus Christ is Lord, to the glory of God the Father" Philippians 2:9-11.***

One of the things that a farmer learns early on is that when harvest time finally comes the real wheat is so heavy with the grain that it has produced that it begins to bow. But the weeds still stand tall and strong. They never bow.

But one of these days every knee is going to bow and every tongue will confess. So you can bow now, or you can bow later. But sooner or later you will bow.

Is there a "Disciple" in the house?
Luke 14:25-33

Introduction

Salvation is free but discipleship is not. Did you catch that? Salvation is free discipleship, the following of Jesus Christ, is not. Christ said, and I quote, "So no one can become my disciple without giving up everything for me." What a statement, any one of you who does not give up everything he has cannot be my disciple.

We don't preach on that enough do we? We preach on salvation that's given so free, but we don't preach on the cost of serving Christ. We have probably read these eight verses a dozen times, maybe more but somehow this concept of giving up everything we own seems to apply to others. "well that's fine for them but Jesus wouldn't expect that of me, would he?"

You say "But hold it Pastor, what if I don't want to be a disciple, what if I just want to be a plain, ordinary, everyday, average Christian?" Well it shouldn't take long in reading the New Testament to discover that Christ doesn't want plain ordinary, everyday, average Christians.

We have come to the place where we want to divide Christians into a couple of different categories. "You see pastor there are your nominal Christians, they're your "CME Christians", you know what I mean, you see them on Christmas, Mother's Day, and Easter! Then there are your Christian Christians, that's what most of us are you know just your average, every day, semi-committed Christian, then there are the disciples, you know what I mean, those super saints. They pray more, they give more they are more disciplined."

The only problem with this theory is that disciple simply means one who follows a teacher or leader. A communist is a disciple of Marx, a Buddhist is a disciple of Buddha, a Moslem is a disciple of Mohammed. And so by definition if you profess to follow Christ then you are a, you ready for it, you are a disciple of Jesus Christ.

Now with that out of the way let's go back to **Luke 14:33, "So no one can become my disciple without giving up everything for me."** Christ is saying, anyone of you who does not give up everything he has cannot be his disciple. You okay?

You say "Yeah but pastor you don't really think that is what he meant do you?" I don't know, how many different meanings could there be to that statement, 'So no one can become my disciple without giving up everything for me.' Sure sounds like that's what he meant to me. "But everything pastor?" well that's what the book says, and we know that we don't debate the book, right?

Let's start at **verse 25**, these are the last days of Christ, and as he makes his way to Jerusalem and his final sacrifice the crowds push in and gather around to hear the teachings of this young influential rabbi.

And as Christ turns and sees the multitude pressing around him, I wonder what thoughts crossed his mind, here are his followers, those who seek to learn from him and they expect great wisdom to come forth from his lips. What will they hear, "Blessed be the peacemakers" "Love your neighbors", "Do unto others" "Love God". What great insight would come forth from the mouth of Jesus?

But no the words of Christ were unlike any others they had ever heard from the master, in *Luke 14:26 "If anyone comes to Me and does not hate his father and mother, wife and children, brothers and sisters, yes, and his own life also, he cannot be My disciple."*

That must have floored them; I would suspect that for what seemed like eternity that those pressing in tight around Jesus just stood in stunned silence. Who could believe that the one who had spoken so eloquently about love could change his tune so completely? What an about face, he's gone from love your enemies, to hate your mother. Love those you barely know, and hate those you know best? What could possibly, have provoked this radical shift in perspective?

I mean let's face it; he's not discussing something that's relatively insignificant, if you're going to love Whoppers with cheese you are going to hate Big Macs. No problem. But he's not talking about trivial things, he's not even talking about in-laws, he's talking about flesh and blood, he's talking about, "I carried you for nine months, my feet swelled to the size of bedroom slippers, and I was in heavy labor for a week and a half." that's what Christ was talking about.

But he probably isn't saying here that we need to consciously hate all that is dear to us read it again this time in the **New Living Translation** *Luke 14:26 " If you want to be my follower you must love me more than your own father and mother, wife and children, brothers and sisters—yes, more than your own life. Otherwise, you cannot be my disciple."*

This statement then is not one of affection as much as it is one of loyalty, to whom do we owe our primary allegiance, to our family or to Christ, to our friends or to Christ, to ourselves or to Christ?

The premise is laid down in **_Matthew 6:24 "No one can serve two masters. For you will hate one and love the other, or be devoted to one and despise the other. You cannot serve both God and money."_**

And for that matter the true disciple cannot serve God and his job, or God and his family, or God and himself. If God is not in first place then God is in the wrong place.

Now don't get me wrong, this doesn't mean that we neglect our family or our friends. And it doesn't mean that we develop a negative self-image, but it does mean that God has to take first place in our life, you okay?

You say "but Preacher my family is a priority, and my job is a priority and my friendships are a priority." Christ tells us in **_Matthew 6:33_** and he will give you all you need from day to day if you live for him and make the Kingdom of God your primary concern. As you draw closer to God, and become more Christ like then you become a better father, or mother, a better husband or wife, a better employee or employer, and a better friend.

In a marriage situation if both partners are aiming for a common goal as they get closer to the goal they draw closer together. Christ will reward faithfulness but in the same breath it is up to you to be faithful. And so as a disciple we will need to be faithful with all that God has given us, and what is it that God has given us? That's simply, all that we have and all that we are. That's the secret to understand tithing; we will never give cheerfully as long as we think we are giving God 10% of what is ours. Instead we need to realize that he is allowing us to keep 90% of what is his.

Our family, our friends, our job our health, our money, our talents, everything we have has been given to us by God and all he asks of us is that we put him ahead of the things which he has given us.

What would happen if you found out that Christ was coming to dinner some night next week? Well you know what would happen. You would have the very best meal possible. You wouldn't take him out to the Golden Arches you'd would you? Man we'd break out the fine china and good silver, linen napkins instead of the usual paper towels. Perhaps a sirloin tip roast with Yorkshire pudding, candied carrots, broccoli with cheese sauce, and for dessert flaming cherry jubilee. Are you all right? You did have breakfast didn't you? I mean if we knew that Jesus was coming to supper we would really outdo ourselves, and I for one would never question the need to do that. What I do question is this; if we would be so conscious of what we would serve Christ at one meal why are we so content with serving him leftovers the rest of the time.

From our money, to our time to our talents we fudge on giving Christ the very best and instead are content to offer him what little we have left over at the end of the week, and that of course is dependent on whether or not we need it. And that doesn't sound like the words of Christ in **Luke 14:33, *"So no one can become my disciple without giving up everything for me."***

But you say "Pastor it's not easy to tithe, and it's not easy to give God precious time out of a day that's already too short." I know that, and you know that and God knows that. But you wanna know something else as well? He never once said that it was going to be easy. You see Christianity was never intended to be a cake walk.

Too many of us have fallen prey to a false theology which proclaims that Christianity will smooth all the humps out of life and will make us healthy, wealthy and wise. "Praise God I've been saved and sanctified and since Jesus came into my life he has made things so much easier, I've gotten a better job, I'm never sick, my children are always polite and pleasant and my marriage is like heaven here on earth." The problem with that is when things start going wrong, and trust me sooner or later things will go wrong, and then we figure that we must have sinned for God to be punishing us.

Well on that beautiful spring day, as the crowds pushed and shoved to be near Christ he turned around and said, "I beg your pardon, I never promised you a rose garden." well maybe that isn't exactly what he said but it was pretty close because in **Luke 14:27** He said, ***"And you cannot be my disciple if you do not carry your own cross and follow me."***

Now that don't sound like a day in the park, but it does sound like commitment, or dare I say "discipleship." If we are going to be the type of Christian that Christ wants us to be it will have to affect our entire life. Christianity isn't just a ticket to heaven it is supposed to be a lifestyle. It isn't just supposed to affect our behavior on Sunday morning; it is supposed to have a direct, dramatic impact on our entire life, Monday through Sunday, day in and day out, 24 hours a day; it is supposed to be a life changing experience.

But why do I sometimes get the feeling that the only difference it makes in some peoples' lives is that it gives them someplace to go between ten thirty and eleven thirty on Sunday mornings, when we don't have something better to do.

Let's be serious, do you really think that Christ came to this earth, lived for thirty three years, suffered the indignities he went through and died on a cross so you could come to church Sunday morning, throw a five dollar bill in the box and then squeak into heaven when you die.

That level of commitment wasn't what he expected two thousand years ago when he called men and women to follow him and it's not what he expects today.

To be truthful it really bugs me when I know that someone professes to follow Christ, professes to love God, but have a commitment level of absolutely zero. It's kind of like the fellow who wrote the note to his girlfriend that said, "For you I'd cross deserts, swim oceans, I'd climb mountains and ford raging rivers, for you I'd fight starving animals. PS. If it's raining on Saturday I won't be over."

The question that each one of us needs to ask is this, "What does God expect of me?" in actual fact it doesn't' matter whether you ever live up to what I expect of you, and it really isn't all that important whether or not you live up to the expectations of this church or this Denomination but it will matter for eternity how you measure up in God's eyes. Your entire life needs to be lived asking the question "what does God want of me?"

The number one resource material for answering that question is the book, His word, and here is a deep thought -- if you don't read it, you will never know what's in it. His word provides the direction that we need as his disciple, but only if we read it.

100 years ago Charles Sheldon wrote the classic "In His Steps" and in the book a number of people make a commitment to ask the question "What would Jesus do?" as they are presented with various issues in their lives. What do you think, do you think that that concept would change your life very much, "What would Jesus do?" What will YOU do?

If nothing is wrong with the "Church" as built by Christ, then the problem has to be with the people inside the church. This is investigated in Chapter Five.

Chapter Five

Wolves in Sheep's Clothing

"Beware of false prophets, which come to you in sheep's clothing, but inwardly they are ravening wolves" (Matt. 7:15).

Jesus gives this solemn warning to the church about those who appear to be from God, but in reality are false prophets from Satan. It was determined previously that there is no problem with the *Church* that Christ built, but instead the problem lies with the people inside who make up the church. The problem starts with the leadership, the pastor.

True and False Prophets

True and false prophets were plainly on the scene both in Israel and in the early church, and present-day experiences of deception are vividly explained and illustrated in the Bible. There are many warnings in the Bible concerning false prophets.

The Old Testament contains examples of false prophets:

- The ones who spoke after *"the deceit of their own heart" (Jer. 14:13-14)*;
- Those who without real prophetic gift borrowed a message and assumed the speech of prophecy *(Jer. 23:28, 31)*;

- And those who sought the prophet's role in order to gain the material gifts which came from the people to their prophets *(Mic. 3:5)*. These, when discovered, were to be punished by death *(Deut. 13:1-5)*.

There were, however, false prophesying from men who honestly believed they had a message from Yahweh. These prophecies from self-deceived prophets often led the people astray. The dream of national greatness was substituted for the voice of Yahweh. It was against such prophesying that the true prophets had to contend. The only test here was the spiritual character of the utterance, and this test demanded a certain moral or spiritual sense which the people did not always possess. Consequently, in times of moral darkness the false prophets, predicting smooth things for the nation, independent of repentance, consecration and the pursuit of spiritual ideals, were honored above the true prophets who emphasized the moral greatness of Yahweh and the necessity of righteousness for the nation *(1 Kings 22:6-12, 2 Chron. 18:5)*.

In New Testament times false prophesying did much injury to the church. Jesus warned the church about false prophets. Careful study of the prophecies concerning the events leading up to the return of the Lord Jesus Christ leads many to believe that they are being fulfilled in this generation, and it is therefore quite surprising that the Church takes very little note of the warnings given about these deceivers.

Marking the Enemy
Romans 16:17-20

Introduction

The apostle having endeavored by his endearing salutations to unite them together, it was not improper to subjoin a caution to take heed of those whose principles and practices were destructive to Christian love. And we may observe:

- **The caution itself, which is given in the most obliging manner that could be:** *"I beseech you, brethren."* He does not will and command, as one that lorded it over God's heritage, but for love's sake beseeches. How earnest, how endearing, are Paul's exhortations! He teaches them,

To see their danger: <u>Mark those who cause divisions and offences</u>.

Our Master had himself foretold that divisions and offences would come, but had entailed a woe on those by whom they come (**Matt 18:7**), and against such we are here cautioned. Those who burden the church with dividing and offending impositions, who uphold and enforce those impositions, who introduce and propagate dividing and offending notions, which are erroneous or justly suspected, who out of pride, ambition, affectation of novelty, or the like, causelessly separate from their brethren, and by perverse disputes, censures, and evil surmising, alienate the affections of Christians one from another-these cause divisions and offences, contrary to, or different from (for that also is implied, it is *para ten didachen),* the doctrine which we have learned. Whatever varies from the form of sound doctrine which we have in the scriptures opens a door to divisions and offences. If truth be once deserted, unity and peace will not last long.

Now, mark those that thus cause divisions, *skopein.* Observe them, the method they take, the end they drive at. There is need of a piercing watchful eye to discern the danger we are in from such people; for commonly the pretenses are plausible, when the projects are very pernicious. Do not look only at the divisions and offences, but run up those streams to the fountain, and mark those that cause them, and especially that in them which causes these divisions and offences, those lusts on each side whence come these wars and fighting. A danger discovered is half prevented.

To shun it:

"Avoid them". Shun all necessary communion and communication with them, lest you be leavened and infected by them. Do not strike in with any dividing interests, nor embrace any of those principles or practices which are destructive to Christian love and charity, or to the truth which is according to godliness.- - Their word will eat as doth a canker." Some think he especially warns them to take heed of the judaizing teachers, who, under convert of the Christian name, kept up the Mosaical ceremonies, and preached the necessity of them, who were industrious in all places to draw disciples after them, and whom Paul in most of his epistles cautions the churches to take heed of.

Reasons to enforce this caution

Because of the pernicious policy of these seducers, (***Romans 16: 18)***, the worse they are, the more need we have to watch against them. Now observe his description of them, in two things:-

The master they serve: not our Lord Jesus Christ.

Though they call themselves Christians, they do not serve Christ; do not aim at his glory, promote his interest, nor do his will, whatever they pretend. How many are there who call Christ Master and Lord, that are far from serving him! But they serve their own belly - their carnal, sensual, secular interests. It is some base lust or other that they are pleasing; pride, ambition, covetousness, luxury, lasciviousness, these are the designs which they are really carrying on. Their God is their belly, (***Phil 3:19)***. What a base master do they serve, and how unworthy to come in competition with Christ, that serve their own bellies, that make gain their godliness, and the gratifying of a sensual appetite the very scope and business of their lives, to which all other purposes and designs must truckle and be made subservient.

The method they take to compass their design -- By good words and fair speeches they deceive the hearts of the simple.

Their words and speeches have a show of holiness and zeal for God (it is an easy thing to be godly from the teeth outward), and show of kindness and love to those into whom they instill their corrupt doctrines, accosting them courteously when they intend them the greatest mischief. Thus by good words and fair speeches the serpent beguiled Eve. Observe, they corrupt their heads by deceiving their hearts, pervert their judgments by slyly insinuating themselves into their affections. We have a great need therefore to keep our hearts with all diligence, especially when seducing spirits are abroad.

Because of the peril we are in, through our proneness and aptness to be inveigled and ensnared by them: *"For your obedience has come abroad unto all men - you are noted in all the churches for a willing, tractable, complying people."*

Therefore, because it was so, these seducing teachers would be the more apt to assault them. The devil and his agents have a particular spite against flourishing churches and flourishing souls. The ship that is known to be richly laden is most exposed to privateers. The adversary and enemy covets such a prey, therefore look to yourselves,

- *2 John v. 8. "The false teachers hear that you are an obedient people, and therefore they will be likely to come among you, to see if you will be obedient to them."*

It has been the common policy of seducers to set upon those who are softened by convictions, and begin to enquire what they shall do, because such do most easily receive the impressions of their opinions. Sad experience witnesses how many who have begun to ask the way to Zion, with their faces thitherward, have fatally split upon this rock, which proves it to be much the duty of ministers, with a double care, to feed the lambs of the flock, to lay a good foundation, and gently to lead those that are with young.

Though it was so, yet they were in danger from these seducers. Paul suggests with a great deal of modesty and tenderness; not as one suspicious of them, but as one solicitous for them: "Your obedience has come abroad unto all men; we grant this and rejoice in it: I am glad therefore on your behalf."

Thus does he insinuate their commendation, the better to make way for the caution. A holy jealousy of our friends may very well comport with a holy joy in them.

- "You think yourselves a very happy people, and so do I too: but for all that you must not be secure: I would have you wise unto that which is good, and simple concerning evil. You are a willing good-natured people, but you had best take heed of being imposed upon by those seducers."

A pliable temper is good when it is under good government; but otherwise it may be very ensnaring; and therefore he gives two general rules:

- **To be wise unto that which is good, that is, to be skillful and intelligent in the truths and ways of God.** *"Be wise to try the spirits, to prove all things, and then to hold fast that only which is good."*

There is need of a great deal of wisdom in our adherence to good truths, and good duties, and good people, lest in any of these we be imposed upon and deluded.

Be ye therefore wise as serpents (*Matt 10:16*), wise to discern that which is really good and that which is counterfeit; wise to distinguish things that differ, to improve opportunities.

While we are in the midst of so many deceivers, we have great need of that wisdom of the prudent which is to understand his way, (***Proverbs 14:8)***.

- **To be simple concerning evil - so wise as not to be deceived, and yet so simple as not to be deceivers.**

It is a holy simplicity, not to be able to contrive, nor palliate, nor carry on, any evil design; akeraious - harmless, unmixed, inoffensive. In malice be you children, *(1 Cor 14:20)*.

The wisdom of the serpent becomes Christians, but not the subtlety of the old serpent. We must withal be harmless as doves. That is a wisely simple man that knows not how to do anything against the truth. Now Paul was the more solicitous for the Roman church, that it might preserve its integrity, because it was so famous; it was a city upon a hill, and many eyes were upon the Christians there, so that an error prevailing there would be a bad precedent, and have an ill influence upon other churches: as indeed it has since proved in fact, the great apostasy of the latter days taking its rise from that capital city.

The errors of leading churches are leading errors. **When the bishop of Rome fell as a great star from heaven (Rev 8:10), his tail drew a third part of the stars after him, Rev 12:4.**

Because of the promise of God, that we shall have victory at last, which is given to quicken and encourage, not superseding, our watchful cares and vigorous endeavors. It is a very sweet promise *(Romans 16:20) The God of peace shall bruise Satan under your feet.*

- **The titles he gives to God: The God of peace, the author and giver of all good.**

When we come to God for spiritual victories, we must not only eye him as the Lord of hosts, whose all power is, but as the God of peace, a God at peace with us, speaking peace to us, working peace in us, creating peace for us. Victory comes from God more as the God of peace than as the God of war; for, in all our conflicts, peace is the thing we must contend for. God, as the God of peace, will restrain and vanquish all those that cause divisions and offences, and so break and disturb the peace of the church.

- **The blessing he expects from God-a victory over Satan.**

If he mean primarily those false doctrines and seducing spirits spoken of before, of which Satan was the prime founder and author, yet doubtless, it comprehends all the other designs and devices of Satan against souls, to defile, disturb, and destroy them, all his attempts to keep us from the purity of heaven, the peace of heaven here, and the possession of heaven hereafter. Satan tempting and troubling, acting as a deceiver and as a destroyer, the God of peace will bruise under our feet. He had cautioned them before against simplicity: now they, being conscious of their own great weakness and folly, might think, "How shall we evade and escape these snares that are laid for us? Will not these adversaries of our souls be at length too hard for us?" "No," says he, "fear not; though you cannot overcome in your own strength and wisdom, yet the God of peace will do it for you; and through him that loved us we shall be more than conquerors."

The victory shall be complete

He shall bruise Satan under your feet, plainly alluding to the first promise the Messiah made in paradise (***Gen 3:15***), that the seed of the woman should break the serpent's head, which is in the fulfilling every day, while the saints are enabled to resist and overcome the temptations of Satan, and will be perfectly fulfilled when, in spite of all the powers of darkness, all that belong to the election of grace shall be brought triumphantly to glory. When Joshua had conquered the kings of Canaan, he called the captains of Israel to set their feet upon the necks of those kings (***Josh 10:24***), so will Christ, our Joshua, enable all his faithful servants and soldiers to set their feet upon Satan's neck, to trample upon, and triumph over, their spiritual enemies. Christ hath overcome for us; disarmed the strong man armed, broken his power, and we have nothing to do but to pursue the victory and divide the spoil. Let this quicken us to our spiritual conflict, to fight the good fight of faith-we have to do with a conquered enemy, and the victory will be perfect shortly.

The victory shall be speedy: He shall do it shortly.

- Yet a little while, and he that shall come will come. He hath said it, Behold, I come quickly.

When Satan seems to have prevailed, and we are ready to give up all for lost, then will the God of peace cut the work short in righteousness. It will encourage soldiers when they know the war will be at an end quickly, in such a victory. Some refer it to the happy period of their contentions in true love and unity; others to the period of the church's persecutions in the conversion of the powers of the empire to Christianity, when the bloody enemies of the church were subdued and trampled on by Constantine, and the church under his government.

It is rather to be applied to the victory which all the saints shall have over Satan when they come to heaven, and shall be forever out of his reach, together with the present victories which through grace they obtain in earnest of that.

Hold out therefore, faith and patience, yet a little while; when we have once got through the Red Sea, we shall see our spiritual enemies dead on the shore, and triumphantly sing the song of Moses and the song of the Lamb. To this therefore he subjoins the benediction, the grace of our Lord Jesus Christ be with you - the good-will of Christ towards you, the good work of Christ in you. This will be the best preservative against the snares of heretics, and schematics, and false teachers.

If the grace of Christ be with us, who can be against us so as to prevail? Be strong therefore in the grace which is in Christ Jesus. Paul, not only as a friend, but as a minister and an apostle, who had received grace for grace, thus with authority blesses them with this blessing.

Satan knows his days are numbered and the Apostle Paul warned us clearly against this cunning enemy who would even disguise himself as *'an angel of light' (2 Cor. 11:14).* Some expect Satan's counterfeit today to be more cunning and devious than in previous history. While this has not yet been seen, we should expect the anti-Christ to live up to the warnings given in Scripture. Who can say for sure how far from power this foul creature may be at this time.

There are many watchmen who have seen Satan blinding and deceiving the saints, within their own fellowships and in other fellowships and denominations and have been amazed at the naïveté of Christians. The gift of discernment of spirits (*1 Cor. 2:10*) has never been needed more than it is now, but if Christians would carefully read the Bible and prayerfully reflect on the Scriptures then many believers would be saved from the snare of Satan and a lot of sadness and heartache would be avoided.

One of the problems with the Laodicean church was their arrogant belief that they could not be deceived. They seriously thought that only those who are unstable, or immature, the 'ignorant and unsuspecting,' could be deceived and led astray. This is also reflected in their poor evangelism, both to the patently unsaved and to those whom they deem to have followed 'another gospel'.

The lukewarm church of today shows little zeal or love for the lost. Sadly, like a "good" counterfeit dollar, the counterfeit is always designed to look exactly like the genuine article. Spiritual counterfeit is no exception, and not only may it require close examination to reveal its true nature, but failure to detect the counterfeit can also have extremely serious and damaging consequences. Confusion, discord, disruption of families, divorce, financial loss, nervous and mental disturbances and even premature deaths are some of the tragic results of counterfeit ministries. Such spiritual shortcomings as pride, domination, delusion and even rejection of the faith can also be the direct outcome of deception.

Examples include any ministry that uses the wrong doctrine ("name it and claim it"), has the wrong motives (personal power and control), and uses the wrong leadership that sometimes has deadly results (e.g. Jim Jones, David Koresh).

The Sign of False Prophets

How clearly did Jesus warn His disciples? Looking across at their magnificent temple from the Mount of Olives, away from the crowds, the disciples were eager to know more about the "end times" from Jesus.

- *Matthew 24:3, "And as he sat upon the Mount of Olives, the disciples came unto him privately, saying, Tell us, when shall these things be? and what shall be the sign of thy coming, and of the end of the world?"*

Many today wonder if we are living in the last days and close to the Lord's return. Wars, rumors of wars, famines, earthquakes and an increase in wickedness are well known signs which Jesus predicted for the end times and we see all these taking place in the world today. Are wars, famines, and earthquakes a sure sign that the end times are at hand? Imagine how shocked the disciples were with the answer Jesus gave them.

- *Matthew 24:4 "And Jesus answered and said unto them, Take heed that no man deceive you."*

Of all the signs that were to herald His second coming, the very first one that Jesus mentioned was the sign of deception among believers: the ***sign of false prophets!***

We are all very aware of the dreadful famines, earthquakes, hurricanes, and the senseless wars in our world today. The news media present us with heart-rending pictures of starving children, of devastated cities, towns, villages and countless refugees. The increase in wickedness in our day is beyond dispute. Violence and terrorism are escalating uncontrollably, and the threat of nuclear war remains a constant reminder that we are living in the last days.

Many are happy to identify false prophets with the leaders of other religions, such as Mohammed, the 'prophet' of Islam, Buddha, or the gurus of the Eastern mystical religious movements. Others may have thought of the many so-called 'Christian' cults which continue to multiply alarmingly in our day. For example, the Mormons proudly proclaim that they are the fastest growing 'Christian' religion today. Most Christians feel reasonably confident that they would not be deceived by any of these deceivers and believe that a born-again Christian would be able to discern the obvious errors of Christian Science, Mormonism or Jehovah's Witnesses, and be able to resist the subtle appeal of Transcendental Meditation or other Eastern philosophies!

Of course we should be able to see that their leaders are certainly false messiahs and false prophets, and the countless numbers of people who have followed them have been led far from the truth. But most forget that Jesus was not addressing the multitude when He gave this warning, but **His very own disciples**. He spoke to those who were closest to Him, and who had forsaken all to follow Him when He said, **'See to it that no one leads *you* astray'**.

COUNTERFEIT CHRISTIANITY
I John 2:18-29

Introduction

For almost two thousand years of Christianity there have been those who would offer a counterfeit faith as a substitute for the real. In verse 18, John reminds us that the antichrist is coming. According to Nelsons New Illustrated Bible Dictionary (pp 79-80), the antichrist is "a false prophet and evil being who will set himself up against Christ and the people of God in the last days before the second coming.

The term refers to one who stands in opposition to all that Jesus Christ represent." Many see the prefix "anti" and say that it refers to "one who is against Christ." While this may be ultimately true, perhaps the real idea of the word is "substitute." The Antichrist is one who offers himself as a substitute for Christ.

Only John uses the title "Antichrist." Other Biblical writers use different terms to describe this diabolical person.
- Daniel refers to the "prince who is to come" in ***Daniel 9:27.***
- Paul calls him the "man of sin" or the "man of lawlessness" in ***2 Thessalonians 2:3.***
- John calls him the "beast out of the sea" in ***Revelation 13:1-10***

However, John's real concern in this present passage is not just for "the antichrist" that is yet to come, but to the existence of the "many antichrists" that were then present in the world. The **"many antichrists"** is a reference to the Gnostic teachers that were beginning to undermine Biblical Christianity near the end of the first century.

I have never known a time when there are more evidences of counterfeit Christianity than in our day. The counterfeit movements are not trying to begin new works from scratch. Rather they are trying to deceive true believers by pulling them away from the true faith. In *verse I John 2:26*, John writes, *"These things have I written unto you concerning them that seduce you."* The Amplified Version puts it this way, *"I write this to you with reference to those who would deceive you [seduce and lead you astray]."*

Many are being deceived by the false teachers that abound today. Christianity is under attack like never before. How can we recognize the real and the false? John gives us several characteristics of counterfeit Christianity, as well as several characteristics of true Christianity.

Characteristics of counterfeit Christianity

There are at least three characteristics of counterfeit Christianity presented in these verses.

- **They have departed from the fellowship** *I John 2:19, "They went out from us, but they were not of us; for if they had been of us, they would no doubt have continued with us; but they went out, that they might be made manifest that they were not all of us."*

Counterfeit Christianity does not come from without, but from within the church. Charles T. Russell, founder of the Jehovah's Witnesses, came from Presbyterian, Congregational and 7th Day

Adventist backgrounds. Moon began with the Presbyterian Church. Joseph Smith, founder of the Mormons was disillusioned with all churches so he founded his own. The leader of the Heaven's Gate cult was a former Presbyterian. They went out from us, but the truth is they were never really part of us at all.

- **They have denied the faith (*I John 2:21-22*), *"I have not written unto you because ye know not the truth, but because ye know it, and that no lie is of the truth. Who is a liar but he that denieth that Jesus is the Christ? He is antichrist, that denieth the Father and the Son."***

Many in the 21st century find it easy to talk about God but difficult to talk about Jesus. There are more and more instances where people are being told that they cannot pray in the name of Jesus. What would you do? One of the chief characteristics of a cult is the denial or the depreciation of the person and work of the Lord Jesus Christ. This passage reveals that to deny Jesus is to deny the Father also.

Some groups such as the Gnostics, the Christian Scientists, New Agers, Unity, etc., deny the humanity of Jesus. That is, Jesus only seemed to be real. Other groups such as the Jehovah's Witnesses deny the deity of Jesus Christ. In reality, all counterfeit Christianity denies the incarnation.

Recent years has witnessed the intensification of attacks on the person and work of Jesus Christ. For example, the Jesus Seminar is comprised of pseudo-scholars. The Jesus Seminar denies that Jesus was the Son of God, his virgin birth, his miracles, his vicarious atonement, and his bodily resurrection. According to the Bible, these people aren't

Christians at all. Yet, many TV documentaries on the Scripture constantly refer to the members of the Jesus Seminar as scholars.

References to true Bible scholarship are minuscule. Modern Gnosticism as presented by The DiVinci Code also rejects Christ. Note what John says about the one who denies that Jesus is the Christ. (*I John 2:22)*, John identifies this person as **"the liar"** and **"the antichrist."** *"He is antichrist, that denieth the Father and the Son"* John declares, *"Whoseover denieth the Son, the same hath not the father" (I John 2:23a).*

- **They deceive the faithful (*I John 2:26*)** *"These things have I written unto you concerning them that seduce you."*

The purpose of this section of *I John* is to warn us, regarding those who would deceive us and lead us astray. They are deceptive in that they have the appearance of true Christianity but in reality deny the fundamentals of the faith.

Characteristics of true Christianity

The best way to recognize counterfeit Christianity is to know true Christianity. A friend of mine had a money changing business in Costa Rica. One day I asked him if he had ever received counterfeit money. When he said that he had, I asked him how he knew the difference. He answered, "I know the difference because I handle the real. I can be counting money without even looking at it, and immediately recognize a counterfeit bill." If we are to guard against counterfeit Christianity we need to know the real. What are the characteristics of real Christianity?

- **Real Christianity is characterized by an acknowledgment of the Son of God.** *"He that acknowledgeth the Son hath the Father also" (I John 2:23b).*

The best way to defend against the cults is to know the Jesus of Scripture. One characteristic of a cult is that they deviate in some way or another from what the Bible teaches about Jesus Christ. For example, the Jehovah's witnesses deny the deity of Jesus Christ. They teach that Jesus was a good man, even a prophet, but he is not God in the flesh. Moreover, the Jehovah's witnesses deny the bodily resurrection of Jesus Christ.

Real Christianity teaches that God was in Christ reconciling the world to Himself. John writes to prove that Jesus is all he claims to be, fully God and fully man. This is the incarnation. Jesus was sinless. He was tempted as we are yet without sin. He is the atoning sacrifice for all our sins. He shed His blood for us on the cross *(I John 2:2)*. Moreover, Jesus rose again from the dead and has been exalted to the Father's right hand.

On the other hand, the antichrist spirit of the Gnostic teachers continues to reject and belittle the person and work of Jesus Christ. The Jesus of the Gnostics, the Jesus Seminar, the New Age movement, and The DiVinci Code is not the Jesus of the Bible. Apart from knowing Jesus Christ as Lord and Savior, these people are eternally lost. All peoples need to know Jesus as Savior and Lord.

- **Real Christianity is characterized by an abiding in the word of God** *(I John 2:24-26)* *"Let that therefore abide in you, which ye have heard from the beginning. If that which ye have heard* *from the beginning shall remain in you, ye also shall continue in the Son, and in the Father. And this is the promise that he hath promised us, even eternal life. These things have I written unto you concerning them that seduce you."*

What had they heard from the beginning? They heard the gospel, the good news of Jesus. The so-called "Gnostic Gospels" supposedly contain additional information about Jesus Christ. However, those books were written long after the events recorded in the Bible. One of the reasons why so many professing Christians are being deceived today is that they do not know the true Word of God. We are to abide in the Word. *Jesus said, "If ye abide in me, and my words abide in you, ye shall ask what ye will, and it shall be done unto you" (John 15:7).*

- **Real Christianity is characterized by the anointing of the Holy Spirit** *(I John 2:20, 27) "But ye have an unction (anointing) from the Holy One, and ye know all things"*

    Verse 27 "But the anointing which ye have received of him abideth in you, and ye need not that any man teach you; but as the same anointing teacheth you of all things, and is truth, and is no lie, and even as it hath taught you, ye shall abide in him"

Every true believer has the Holy Spirit living in his life. Paul wrote, *"Now if any man have not the Spirit of Christ, he is none of his" (Romans 8:9)*. Paul went on to write, *"The Spirit Himself beareth witness with our spirit, that we are the children of God" (Romans 8:16).*

The anointing in this passage is the anointing of the Holy Spirit that is available for every true believer in Jesus Christ. Such anointing sets the believer apart to God, enables us to know the truth, and equips us for ministry.

Beware of the counterfeit Christianity. Don't let the devil deceive you by pulling you away from true Biblical Christianity. *(I John 2:28), "And now, little children, abide in Him; that, when he shall appear, we may have confidence, and not be ashamed before him at his coming."*

John 6:66 the Bible says, "From that time many of His disciples went back and walked with Him no more." But Jesus asked his disciples "Do you also want to go away?" Peter, speaking for all the disciples asked, "Lord, to whom shall we go? You have the words of eternal life. Also we have come to believe and know that you are the Christ the Son of the living God."

John wrote in *III John 4, "I have no greater joy than to hear that my children walk in truth."* John was expressing the heart of the Lord Jesus in these words. Don't be deceived by the counterfeit. Keep your eyes on Jesus. Abide in Him. Remain in him.

Tell your soul that you want the real deal, the real McCoy. Tell your soul and tell the world you want JESUS THE SON OF THE LIVING GOD!!!!!

Today, many Christians belonging to Bible believing churches and fellowships are being exposed to teaching not only from their own pastor, or elders, but also from a wide variety of visiting ministers and preachers. To make this matter even worse is the fact that speakers not only travel widely, but also often have radio and television programs, and publish their own literature, ensuring nation-wide and often world-wide publicity. But Scripture clearly reveals that, if you continue to rub shoulders with those whom God has exposed and judged, you are likely to share in their fate!

- Jonathan knew his father, Saul, was a demonized murderer of the priesthood (*1 Sam. 22*), yet remained in his army and eventually shared in his fate (*1 Sam. 31*) on Mount Gilboa.

Many of these preachers declare an 'anointing' of power, sometimes with 'signs and miracles,' and with an appealing ("ear tickling") message. They may tell impressive stories of 'what God has done' through their ministries, and introduce new teachings and revelations to their unquestioning hearers but: *are they all of God?*

We should heed the warning *in 2 Timothy 4:3:* *"For the time will come when they will not endure sound doctrine; but wanting to have their ears tickled, they will accumulate for themselves teachers in accordance to their own desires."*

Don't Condone what God Condemns!
I Samuel 2: 12, 22-25; 3: 11-14

Introduction

We live in a world today where it is harder than ever to be a Christian. Jesus taught in the Bible that when a man curses or uses profanity it is a sign of evil that was in that man's heart. It is popular today for both men and women to curse. Popular movies and TV are responsible for causing society to accept foul language as the "norm." We have been conditioned to be "politically correct" and to be more tolerant to others even when we know it's wrong. We have priests who tell us to accept homosexuals, to give sin a new name, a disease.

We are going to look at a cursed family, where the children were sinning and yet the father looked the other way. We will also look to our heavenly Father who loves and forgives us.

Sinful Children

In our text today we find that the sons of Eli, Phinehas and Hophni, were sinning out of control. (*I Samuel 2:12-25),* we are told that they were preachers and yet they were sinning openly as if they had no shame. They profaned the offerings of the Lord, and made a gain to themselves, or rather a gratification of their own luxury, out of them. They would eat the sacrificial meat before it would be dedicated to God. They robbed those who gave offerings, and seized for themselves some of their part of the sacrifice of the peace-offerings. They stepped in before God himself, and encroached upon His right too.

They would even have sex with the women who worked at the church! (*I Samuel 2:22*) These are preachers! What do you think the people were thinking? Eli hears of all this and in **verses 23-25a** he *tries* to correct them, but in **verse 25b** they don't pay him any attention. Eli had two terrible sons, priests or not; they were evil and disobeyed their father.

Now let's look at Eli. Eli was a high priest and judge. In **verse 22;** we are told the Eli was very old. In fact Eli was 98 and was just about blind. He had given the duties of the church to his sons and they abused it terribly. Now Eli hears of the sins being committed by his sons and tells them that they are wrong. However, it's too little, too late. In **verse 25b** they ignore him. That's why in **Proverbs 22:6** we are told to, **"Train up a child in the way he should go; and when he is old, he will not depart from it."** You see, Eli knew all along that his sons were sinning; he **chose** to ignore it until he couldn't anymore. **Prov. 19:18** says, **"Chasten thy son while there is hope, and let not thy soul spare for his crying."** Eli waited too late to try to correct his sons, they were now grown adults and simply ignored their father. But every sin sowed will be reaped.

Look at *I Samuel 3:11*, God tells Samuel that He is going to punish the house of Eli in such a way that every ear in Israel that hears of it will tingle! You don't want to fall into the hands of the living God! In **verse 13** God says that He will judge the house of Eli **forever** because

Eli knew his sons were vile (disgusting, wicked, worthless, degrading), and Eli didn't do anything to restrain them.

The sins of Eli and his sons are so bad that God says in **verse 14** that no sacrifice or offering will purge or clean them from their sins forever. God is angry! Later in battle Eli's two sons are killed while carrying the ark of God and when word reaches him he falls back from his seat and breaks his neck.

Phinehas' wife who is pregnant hears this and goes into labor. She names her son Ichabod, which means**, *"The glory is departed from Israel: for the ark of God is taken."*** *I Samuel 4: 22.*

The Family Now

Now let's look at our children. None of us have children that bad do we? Well, do we? Let's not be like Eli and turn our heads. Today we have the very same situation. Let the school call us and we have to leave our job and go have a meeting with the teacher or the principal. They tell us that our Billie or our Barbara is acting up. Instead of believing them, we believe our child. After all, our children don't lie, do they? That teacher is picking on my child, calling me 2-3 times a week. I raise good children!

Eli thought the same thing. It wasn't until he simply couldn't ignore the sins of his children anymore that he finally spoke up. But do we? Here's how it happens; the first time you threaten your child and you don't follow through with the threat, your child has just started to rule you. That's how the Eli Syndrome begins and if you're not careful, you're going to wind up like Eli.

Parents, what the word of God said to Eli it says to us:

- *Proverbs 22:6* we are told to, *"Train up a child in the way he should go; and when he is old, he will not depart from it."*
- *Proverbs 19:18* says, *"Chasten thy son while there is hope, and let not thy soul spare for his crying."*

Now let's look at the church. Today we as Christians are condoning more sins than ever. What's really upsetting is the growing number of religious people who engage in the practicing of sin and see nothing wrong with it. What practices? How about sex before marriage? The Bible call this fornication, and nowhere is this ever being condoned is when a man and woman live together and are not married. We condone this by saying they are cohabitating. The slang term is "shackin." God condemns it as sin. We condone sex outside of marriage as "a one night stand," "tipping," "creeping," "getting a little on the side." God condemns it as adultery. We condone hearsay as "the 411." God condemns it as gossip. We condone homosexuality as "alternative lifestyles." God condemns it as an abomination. We condone sin by saying, "Well I don't see anything wrong with it." Turn to *Proverbs 14:12* and *Proverbs. 16:25.* Read. God condemns sin. **Don't condone what God condemns!**

I know of a mother who gave her daughter the juice during a communion service because the mother didn't like grape juice. Now that was bad enough, but when the mother's grandmother heard of it she said that it was all right! **Don't condone what God condemns!!**

- *I Corinthians 6:9-10*. These people will not inherent the kingdom of God. Are you in this group?

Our Heavenly Father

In *I Corinthians 6:11,* we are told that we, Christians, are washed, sanctified, and justified by the blood of Jesus and by the Spirit of God. Have you been washed in the blood of the crucified Lamb? Have you been sanctified, sat aside by our Lord and Savior Jesus Christ? Have you been justified by the Spirit of God? I know Him! Do you know Him? Jesus loves you. He died for you. **Don't condone what God condemns!!!**

Conclusion

Today we looked at what happens when we condone the sins of our family, our church, and ourselves. God hates the sin, but He loves the sinner. He wants all of us, His children to be washed, sanctified, and justified. God bless you.

Saturday Night Sinner and Sunday Morning Saint

Revelations 3:14-19

Introduction

One of the most frightening groups of verses in the Bible is found in **Revelations 3:14-19**, when Christ is talking to the Church of Laodicea. He is addressing the people of a city known for its wealth. But despite its financial prosperity, it was spiritually impoverished.

He says to the people "You are neither cold nor hot." I wish that you were either cold or hot. So because you are lukewarm, and neither cold nor hot, I am about to spit you out of My mouth. For you say 'I am rich, I have prospered, and I need nothing.' You don't realize that you are wretched, pitiable, poor, blind, and naked."

What's frightening about this statement is that a lot of people in this world who call themselves Christians are lukewarm. They fall into the category of sometime or part time Christian. Yes we might go to church on Sundays, make an appearance, and think to ourselves, hey, I don't sell drugs, I haven't killed anybody, I never robbed a bank, I even give to charities. But the real question is have I given myself completely to God? Am I a sometime, part time or full time Christian?

Let's first of all consider what lukewarm is. Not hot and not cold, not even warm, just a little past cool. When you cook food, you have to apply heat. Imagine what fried chicken would taste like if we cooked it in lukewarm grease. It would be something that wouldn't reach the mouth to throw up! Well when we are not committed to God, and live according to what we think rather than how He commands, we fall into the same trap that the church of Laodicea fell into.

We will break this down into three categories. The truth be known, we could actually add two more categories…"all of the above, or none of the above."

A Sometime Christian

A sometime Christian would be a fair-weather Christian, a Christian of convenience. Goes to church every Sunday but never applies what is learned. Content is saying "I go to church," but refuses to read the word of God, to pray on a continuous basic, do anything that may take away from his or her normal schedule. But in **Matthew 23:4,** it describes them to a 'T'

- ***"For they bind heavy burdens and grievous to be borne, and lay them on men's shoulders; but they themselves will not move them with one of their fingers."***

These sometime Christians can recite what has been preached to them, but are unwilling to apply it to their own lives, but they can tell you how your life should be led. "Girl if I were you I would do it this way…. "Man if you asked me I would work it that way…." But if you ask what are they going to do…. Well the response is usually "I don't know, or nothing right now, or I'm not ready yet….. etc…." But the word of God does not support this mindset; in fact the text for today gives us an understanding just how distasteful it is to God that we do not give Him our all.

Consider worship. So many people believe worship is the slow "Dr. Watts" songs we hate to sing on Sunday morning. Others have the mindset that it is going to church on Sunday morning. **But worship is a way of life that brings glory and honor to God.** Worship is being obedient to God when it is uncomfortable. Worship is praising God when things are not going right. Worship is finding good in a situation and refraining from grumbling and mumbling about what "ain't right".... Because to tell the truth, stuff "ain't right" because of something we did or didn't do!

But in order to elevate from a sometime Christian, we must be willing to enter into the holy of holies and spend time with a holy God.

- *(Hebrews 10:19-22), "19 Having therefore, brethren, boldness to enter into the holiest by the blood of Jesus, 20 By a new and living way, which he hath consecrated for us, through the veil, that is to say, his flesh; 21 And having an high priest over the house of God; 22 Let us draw near with a true heart in full assurance of faith, having our hearts sprinkled from an evil conscience, and our bodies washed with pure water."*

Therefore, brothers and sisters, since we have confidence to enter the Most Holy Place by the blood of Jesus, by a new and living way opened for us through the curtain, that is, his body, and since we have a great high priest over the house of God, let us draw near to God with a sincere heart in full assurance of faith, having our hearts sprinkled to cleanse us from a guilty conscience and having our bodies washed with pure water.

A true worship! This is not something exclusively for Sunday morning. This is not some ritual that becomes tedious as time goes by. This is the real deal, coming each day with a level of expectancy. Expecting God to move. Expecting God to act. Expecting God to make a way. Expecting God to bless. Expecting God to do something. But a sometime Christian has no level of expectancy, because they have no connection to God, just a knowledge that there is one.

Part time Christian

Now they are a little better than a sometime Christian. There is a level of prayer time. There is some bible time here there and somewhere. However, a part time Christian picks and chooses what they will or will not do for God. "I will go to bible study, but I won't fast. I'll fast, but I'm not reading the word on a daily basis. I'll read the word every day, but I'm not going to accept my call. I'll get to church every Sunday, but I won't be on time. I'll be on time, but I'm not doing all that praise and worship cause it don't take all that. I'll do praise and worship, but I won't testify, cuz everybody don't need to know my business."

A part time Christian is only willing to do it part of the way. But *Isaiah 29:13* states,

- *"Wherefore the Lord said, Forasmuch as this people draw near me with their mouth, and with their lips do honour me, but have removed their heart far from me, and their fear toward me is taught by the precept of men:"*

These people honor me with their lips, but their hearts are far from me. They worship me in vain; their teachings are but rules taught by men.

When we simply honor God with our words, "I believe – I trust – I know God will make a way" but our actions give indication that we really don't; He is not pleased...we are still lukewarm....we are still nasty..... we are still like bile in the bowels of the belly of God.

We don't have the option of picking and choosing when our walk is with God. We don't have the option of serving God today and not serving Him tomorrow, we can't be Saturday night sinners and Sunday morning Saints– because the word says**...."Choose ye this day, whom you will serve....but as for me and my house I will serve the Lord!"** It's not a multiple choice...you either trust God or you don't. You either believe that He will take care of you, or you don't. You either believe He is in control or you don't! But the bottom line is that a part time Christian is still a half time believer, and a half time believer cannot reap the total package of benefits God has in store.

Full time Christian

Matthew 4:19 Jesus says *"Follow me and I will make you fishers of men..."* or better yet... Follow me and I will make you into what you ought to be! A full time Christian spends less time looking at what they can see, and more time clinging to what God said would be. This is backed up by *John 14:1, "Let not your heart be troubled: ye believe in God, believe also in me."* Jesus is saying this: "Trust in God and trust in me" --- don't worry about it, I've got this, it's handled because you trust me. Don't stress about it, don't fret about it, I've got this, it's handled – because you trust me.... Don't lay awake at night, stop calling Jack, Joe and Jimmy, stop calling Mary, Martha, and Maggie. I've got this – it's handled – because you trust me!..... There are perks to being full time!

Compare it to a part time worker. Part time workers don't have health insurance, they don't get vacation days, there is no retirement package, and they are the first let go. Full time workers can get cars, bonuses, vacations, sick leave, health insurance, life insurance, some get corner offices. Because they have given themselves totally to the position. Those fulltime employees who abuse their benefits, who don't show up to work, who call in sick excessively, get fired. A full time Christian is not one who only does what is convenient and comfortable, they have given themselves completely to God; committed to do the will of God.

A full time Christian understands **Romans 12:1** and presents themselves as a living sacrifice, willing to go above and beyond what others see as the normal, because they understand that God will give great rewards to those who are true to their purpose. God has promised abundance to those who are faithful in all things.

- *(Matthew 5:1) "Rejoice, and be exceeding glad: for great is your reward in heaven: for so persecuted they the prophets which were before you."*
- *(1 Peter 3:9) "Not rendering evil for evil, or railing for railing: but contrariwise blessing; knowing that ye are thereunto called, that ye should inherit a blessing."*

God promises to take care of those who don't allow other's actions to cause them to act negatively. Do not repay evil with evil or insult with insult, but with blessing, because to this you were called so that you may inherit a blessing

Full time – not sometime

Full time – not half time

Full time - not part time

Full time Christian

Trusting in God even when things seem impossible

Trusting in God even when there seems to be no way

Serving God even when you wish you were doing other things

Praising God even when your soul is weary

Blessing God even when folk around you are trying to tear you down, Praying and trusting God even when your bills far surpass your personal resources, because you have indeed come to understand that God is not a man so He cannot lie!

Full time Christians know to: Read the Word, Pray the Word, Rejoice in the Word, Apply the word, Because there is power in the Word!

No longer looking at things as difficult – but understanding that if God said it would be, then He will make it so. He told you to start a business, He will give you resources, but you got to learn to wait on Him and be of good courage (that means without doubt) and He will renew your strength……..

He told you to pray over your children, not give up on them because they seem too far gone….then do just that ….. tell God, I cast my cares upon you God….. Be my ram…..He told you He would fix your marriage – than stop listening to other folk – cause haters hate to see happiness – instead say – God what you put together – nobody else can break apart!

He told you to step out and work your ministry – so stop making excuses and saying I will tomorrow – cause tomorrow is not promised – instead say Here I am God, everything I am and even everything I'm not, I give myself to you completely…now work in me and through me to make this thing come to pass.

We should be full time, because God is full time to us. He loves us full time. He cares for us full time. He provides for us full time. He does this even when we don't do…. He made a plan for us that would give us full time help. He sent His only begotten son to die for us so we would be saved full time from the gates of hell. He gave us full time help when He empowered us with the Holy Ghost that came to comfort and empower. He gave us full time help when He said when you fall down I will help you get back up again….. So why would we want to be anything but full time. Stop Being a Saturday night sinner and become a full time everyday Saint for the Lord! God bless you!

In the book of Acts churches grew rapidly. *Acts 1:41* tells of about 3000 souls being added to the church. Was this the first "megachurch"? Chapter 6 provides an in-depth examination of the "megachurch".

Chapter Six

The Mega Church

What is a "mega-church"? Technically a mega-church is one that averages over 2,000 people in attendance. That's the draw point, the break-off point for a mega-church, 2,000, not in members, but in attendance on a weekly basis. Now allow this to be put in perspective. In 1963 in America, only 93 churches in America had more than 1,000 people in weekly attendance. Today, there are over 6,000 churches that run over 2,000 in weekly attendance with some churches topping 50,000 plus in America.

There is a shifting. There are 6,000 churches that run over 1,000. There are about 750 churches that run over 2,000; so those are the real mega-churches, the 750 over 2,000. There are about 20 churches in America that run over 10,000 in attendance on a typical weekend, and there are three of them that run over 20,000. At one time the three largest churches in America were Willow Creek Community Church in South Barrington, outside of Chicago; Lakewood Church in Houston, (the only mega-church on television), and Saddleback which was the largest church in America. Saddleback is pastured by Rick Warren of <u>The Purposed Driven Church</u> fame. The church's 25th anniversary was held on Resurrection (Easter) Sunday. He states that he preached 12 sermons in a row to over 45,000 in attendance. For the anniversary service the church rented the Anaheim Angels Baseball Stadium and had 30,000 in attendance. He reports having 82,000 names on the church roll. Those numbers have since changed.

The Top 10 Largest Mega Churches in the United States (*by weekly attendance averages according to Forbes.com*)

- Lakewood Church | Houston, TX
- Second Baptist Church | Houston, TX
- North Point Community Church | Atlanta, GA
- Willow Creek Community Church | Chicago IL
- LifeChurch.tv | Edmond, OK
- West Angeles Church of God in Christ | Los Angeles, CA
- Fellowship Church | Grapevine, TX
- Saddleback Valley Community Church | Lake Forest, Ca.
- Calvary Chapel | Ft. Lauderdale, FL
- The Potter's House | Dallas, TX

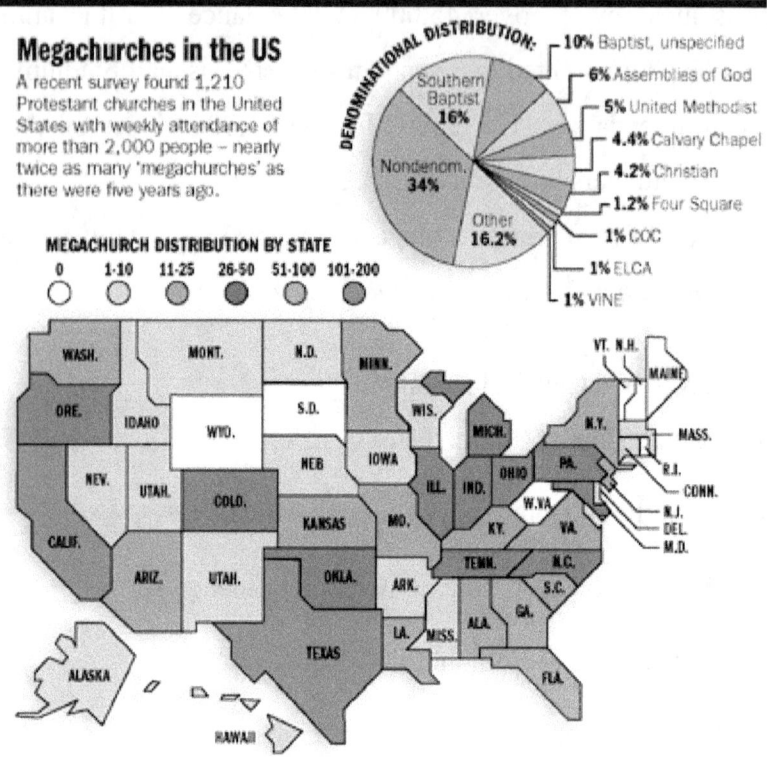

- Most churches within the mega church movement are primarily identified as being Protestant,

- Evangelical, or Pentecostal; but half within the United States are considered non-denominational.

- Although the Roman Catholic Church has a great abundance of churches with 2,000 to 3,000, parishioners, the Catholic Church is not considered to be a part of the mega church phenomenon.

- Historians trace the beginnings of the mega church movement in the United States back to the early 1950's. In 1970, there were considered to be only 50 mega churches. Today there are more than 1,300 mega churches just within the U.S. In 2005, California led the nation with 178 of them, followed by 157 in Texas and 85 in Florida, according to the book *Beyond Megachurch*

- *Myths: What We Can Learn From America's Largest Churches* (Bogan, J., 2009).

Also, the methodology of the mega church has also evolved into something starkly different from the traditional church. Often times referred to and known as "seeker churches," many mega churches focus solely on accommodating primarily to new Christians and religious seekers, rather than to Christians who are already attending services.

Convenience and ease of use are generally the key factors in accommodating most church members. Mega church leadership continually seeks to create activities and programs which will attract the masses. It is safe to say that many mega churches are market driven and user friendly because every detail down to which type of songs will be sung and the type of music that will be played is tailored to seeking and retaining new membership. You would be very hard pressed to find any mega church's choir or current membership singing "I'll Fly Away" or "Jesus is Real" at any of the many conveniently scheduled services.

Many hire and retain the services of professional musicians and songwriting teams to construct generic, easy to digest song catalogs for church use during services. Not only does the consumer get to sing fresh and catchy songs, but also those same songs can be recorded and sold to the public. Being able to offer a seemingly unique experience is a major objective of the mega church.

The target and mission of the mega church is to reach the unchurched and not the unsaved. Its focus is more on the consumer's mentality than the consumer's heart and the actual teachings of Jesus. Marketing has become so important to the mega church that anything that can be perceived as inconvenient to the consumer has to be removed. The overall aesthetic of the mega church starting with the entrance of the church to the pastor is all market driven. These churches utilize business marketing principles to "sell" the church program and accompanying related products to the masses.

Actual salvation is just an afterthought if it is a thought at all. Just like a corporation, the mega church seeks to provide only a product that will meet the real or perceived needs of the consuming public and Jesus is not the real product. Entertainment is and has become the focal point with the religion trailing third to the pastor.[9]

Can a Church get "Too Big"?

When a church grows to such a size that it becomes a corporation, it has lost sight of the community. In some churches the pastor is the preaching machine while someone else runs the business side. In other churches the pastor is the CEO, the boss, the chairman of the board. But in both cases the pastor is a corporate officer, not a shepherd. For some pastors it becomes too much to bear. One such example is Terry Swicewood, former pastor of the 3,700 member Myers Park Presbyterian Church in Mecklenburg, North Carolina. Swicegood resigned his position as senior pastor in January 1999 because, as he told *The Charlotte Observer,* "I'm a guy with a pastor's heart, and I'm being a CEO."

In a letter to church members, Swicegood said he yearned to be a pastor, a spiritual leader, a teacher, and a friend – but "as presently constituted, the job of senior minister of Myers Park Presbyterian Church requires long and full days of managing, planning and strategizing."

The breaking point for Swicegood came one evening when he looked over a log of his daily activities and realized that he spent eleven of his fourteen hours of work that day in meetings and planning. He told the *Observer*, "I looked down the road to my future and said, 'This is my future.' I just felt absolutely drained. It was a kind of epiphany." [10]

You're in the church. Is the church in you?

II Kings 5:20-27

Introduction

Many people today are wasting their time in church. What I mean by this is that they are in the church but the church is not in them. Amazingly people come to church and see other people get blessed, healed, and delivered but it is never their day for a miracle.

It doesn't make any sense to attend church every week and still die and go to Hell. We should keep in mind that we might not be perfect but we can be in right standing before God.

The text addresses the issue of being around the people of God and not actually being one of them. It is sort of like Lot, the one who was blessed because of Abraham, not because of his standing before God.

Look at the things that Gehazi did that led to his awful punishment at the end of this chapter. He was in the church, but the church was not in him.

NOTICE THE DESIRE OF GEHAZI

II Kings 5:20a

- Gehazi is classified as the Servant of the Man of God *"20 But Gehazi, the servant of Elisha the man of God, said, Behold, my master hath spared Naaman this Syrian, in not receiving at his hands that which he brought..."*

Naaman, a Syrian soldier, had many servants, and we read how wise and good they were, *(II Kings 5:13)*. Elisha, a holy prophet, a man of God, has but one servant and that servant proves to be a base, lying, self-centered man. Elisha, his master refused Naaman's treasures, but he coveted them, he desired them.

COVETOUSNESS

Covetousness is a very grave sin; indeed, so heinous is it that the Scriptures class it among the very gravest and grossest crimes (*Ephesians 5:3*). *Colossians 3:5* it is "idolatry," while in *I Corinthians 6:10* it is set forth as excluding a man from heaven. Its heinousness, doubtless, is accounted for by its being in a very real sense the root of so many other forms of sin, e.g. departure from the faith *I Timothy 6:9-10*; lying *II Kings 5:22-25*; theft *Joshua 7:21*; domestic trouble *Proverbs 15:27*; murder *Ezekiel 22:12*; indeed, it leads to "many foolish and hurtful lusts"

NOTICE THE DECISION OF GEHAZI
II Kings 5:20b-21a

- *"20... but, as the LORD liveth, I will run after him, and take somewhat of him."*

So Gehazi followed after Naaman. When the situation presents itself Gehazi fails the test. Instead of doing God's will he acts and does his Own will because it seems good and harmless (Be careful of good intentions when they are not Godly motivated, they may still equal sin). His lack of faith is displayed in his haste to provide for himself thus not allowing God to provide for his needs (So many of us are the same way, we are quick to take matters into our own hands instead of letting God be God, He knows our needs).

- The love of money is the root of all evil. **Matt. 6:32-33** tells us that the things that the Gentiles seek after we have faith for. **Proverbs 3:5-6** tells us to trust in the LORD. **Philip 4:19** tells us that God shall supply all our need.

He runs to do evil... how often are we quick to do evil and slow to do good.

Notice that Gehazi's covetousness caused him to 'secretly' follow after Naaman. His desire was to obtain or to take away from Naaman something that belonged to Naaman. At first, he had a desire, a thought, now he decides to put it into action. Now he is rushing to Naaman to get his loot.

We Christians often display that same tendency. Something that belongs to someone else, or some talent or ability that is beyond our reach, can seem so much more appealing than what we already possess. Yet the Lord wants us to be satisfied with what He has given to us.

NOTICE THE DECEPTION OF GEHAZI
II Kings 5:21b-22

- *"21...and when Naaman saw him running after him, he lighted down from the chariot to meet him, and said, Is all well? . 22 and he said, All is well. My master hath sent me, saying, Behold, even now there be come to me from mount Ephraim two young men of the sons of the prophets: give them, I pray thee, a talent of silver, and two changes of garments."*

When Naaman, like a person of accomplished manners, lighted from his chariot to meet him (*verse 21*), he told him a deliberate lie, that his master sent him to him.

- He lies on the man on God and thus he is lying on God You may successfully deceive others, but you cannot deceive God.

NOTICE THE DECREE OF NAAMAN
II Kings 5:23

- *"23 And Naaman said, Be content, take two talents. And he urged him, and bound two talents of silver in two bags, with two changes of garments, and laid them upon two of his servants; and they bare them before him."*

His story of the two sons of the prophets was as silly as it was false; if he would have begged a token for two young scholars, surely less than a talent of silver might serve them.

Have you ever heard of a "Silver tongue devil?" That's a person who lies so easily that it sounds like the truth. This is what Gehazi is becoming. Naaman was gracious for what the Prophet of God had done for him thus he didn't question the need.

NOTICE THE DEMAND OF ELISHA
II Kings 5:24-25

- *"24 And when he came to the tower, he took them from their hand, and bestowed them in the house: and he let the men go, and they departed. 25 But he went in, and stood before his master. And Elisha said unto him, Whence comest thou, Gehazi? And he said, Thy servant went no whither."*

Then, after receiving the treasure, he has to hide it by getting rid of Naaman's servants while on the other side of the hill. In a house, behind a hill, where Elisha could not see him, he hid the money and wardrobes Naaman had given him. He would secretly return for the loot later on.

IT FEELS THAT IF NO ONE KNOWS WE MUST BE OK. (How many of us right now are sitting here knowing that we have hidden sin in our lives, but we feel that if no one knows we must be ok.) Lest his absence should be noticed, Gehazi hastened, without being called, to appear before his master. In the East it is usual for servants to remain most of the day in their lord's presence, only quitting it when given some order to execute.

His master asked him where he had been, "Nowhere, sir" (said he), "out of the house." Here comes the Silver Tongue devil again. Note: One lie commonly leads to another and another; the way of that sin is down-hill.

Have you ever asked a friend or a relative for some money and they say, "Man I ain't got no money!" and they're lying through their teeth! The truth is they have some money, but they don't want to give any of it to you!

Gehazi hadn't been spiritually alert and because he hadn't, it had caused him to do evil.

NOTICE THE DECLARATON OF ELISHA
II Kings 5:26

- *"And he said unto him, Went not mine heart with thee, when the man turned again from his chariot to meet thee? Is it a time to receive money, and to receive garments, and oliveyards, and vineyards, and sheep, and oxen, and menservants, and maidservants?"*

Had Gehazi yet to learn that prophets had spiritual eyes? Did he think to hide anything from a seer, from him with whom the secret of the Lord was? How many parents can tell when their child is lying? The same with Elisha.

It was foolish for Gehazi to attempt what he did. Sin blinds people to the real circumstances and consequences with which they have to deal. Above all, it destroys their power of sensing the presence of God.

What Gehazi assumed about Elisha, that is, that he would not find out, all sinners assume about Almighty God, that He will not discover anything. But God does find out, and lying always leads to disgrace.

NOTICE THE DEFILEMENT OF GEHAZI
II Kings 5:27

- *The leprosy therefore of Naaman shall cleave unto thee, and unto thy seed forever. And he went out from his presence a leper as white as snow."*

Gehazi's leprosy was an outward sign of an inward spiritual condition, the fact that Gehazi's moral nature had been permanently damaged. Gehazi could never regain his integrity. He must carry leprosy with him to his grave:

And so Gehazi went to live with the lepers and to mourn for a lifetime the folly and the wickedness which led him to throw away the fellowship and confidence of so great a friend as Elisha.

Conclusion

Jesus gave His life for us on Calvary. We do not have to lie, cheat, or steal to be blessed. God will supply our every need, and when we delight ourselves in Him, He will give us the desires of our hearts.

Corporations vs. Community

There is no loyalty in a corporation. Why? Because it's hard to be loyal to a machine! Could this be why so many people jump from church to church? They don't feel connected. It's hard to leave a community but not at all difficult to leave a corporation. Many people feel that we, the church, have created *The Church, Inc.* Observe the following list and compare the differences between the Corporation and the Community.

Corporation	Community
Programs	People
Money	Ministry
Systems	Salvation
Profits	People
Management	Ministry
Numbers	Nourishment
Product	Purpose

The DANGER of being Unstable
Prov. 24:19-22

Introduction

Today I want to encourage you to stay rooted in the Lord for there is a group of people we need to pray for; the Unstable. Today we're going to look at the Unstable, how to recognize them (they may not even know it themselves), what to warn them about, and how to encourage them to be steadfast.

Characteristics of the Unstable

- **Double minded.** In *James 1:8* we are told that, *"A double minded man is unstable in all his ways."*

Here is a person who prays to God for something and yet does not believe that God can do it. The Bible says that that person is double-minded and is unstable.

- *(Luke 16:13) Jesus* says, *"No servant can serve two masters: for either he will hate the one, and love the other; or else he will hold to the one, and despise the other. Ye cannot serve God and mammon."*

A person who hollers in the club on Saturday night and then shouts "Amen" on Sunday morning is trying to serve two. Jesus says that this cannot be. This person is unstable.

- **Indecision.** In *I Kings 18:21* the prophet Elijah ask the people a question. He says, *"And Elijah came unto all the people, and said, How long halt ye between two pinions? if the LORD be God, follow him: but if Baal, then follow him. And the people answered him not a word."*

Notice that the people didn't answer. See, an unstable person cannot give you a solid answer because they are not sure of the answer.

- **Opinions.** Job 32:6, 10, 17. Elihu speaks to Job and the others and tells them what he thinks.

Warnings against being Unstable

In our text we are told not to worry or be afraid of the evil men. We are told in our key verse, *Proverbs 24:21*, not to <u>meddle</u>, or associate with those who are unstable for in **verse 22** their calamity or judgment shall rise suddenly and no one will be able to know the ruin they suffer.

In *I Corinthians 10:21* we are told that, *"Ye cannot drink the cup of the Lord, and the cup of devils: ye cannot be partakers of the Lord's table, and of the table of devils."* We say this before we serve the Lord's Supper so that no one will bring damnation to their soul. If you're unstable God will bring judgment against you. In *Hosea 10:2* the prophet says, *"Their heart is divided; now shall they be found faulty: he shall break down their altars, he shall spoil their images."*

In *Luke 9:62 Jesus* says, *"...No man, having put his hand to the plough, and looking back, is fit for the kingdom of God."* Jesus is telling us that if we are unstable, if we are double minded, if we want to look back and **go back** to our old ways, then we are not fit for the kingdom of God.

Let me give you some examples of people being unstable or double minded. Peter was one of the 12 disciples and one of the "inner circle" that was made up of Peter, James, and John. It was Peter who witnessed the transformation and said "it is good to be here." It was Peter who walked out on the water to meet Jesus but as soon as he took his eyes off Christ he started to sink. It was Peter who said the Jesus was the Christ, the Son of the living God. And yet it was this same Peter who boasted that he would follow Christ anywhere than Jesus told him he would betray Him three times before the rooster crowed in the morning. Do you not know that it was only **after** Jesus rose from the grave that Peter became steadfast. So what does that tell us about us? We are to be steadfast!

A person who tries to read the Bible with the TV on is unstable. How? Jesus told us that you cannot serve two masters. Anybody who tells you they can read the Bible with the TV or the radio on is an unstable person.

A person who comes to Bible Study and learns something new goes home and talks about it on the phone instead of with the pastor is an unstable person.

An unstable person can be **anybody** in the church. It can be a member jumping from one side of the fence to the other. It can be a deacon who smiles in the pastors face but is trying to get rid of him behind his back. An unstable choir member wants to lead every song.

When they cannot, they get mad, quit the choir, and then talk about everyone else in the choir.

Let me tell you that even pastors can be unstable. A pastor who tries to be "buddy-buddy" with every member, a pastor who's more concerned with the amount of money taken in the offering, a pastor who only preaches "feel good" sermons instead of the Word of God is an unstable preacher who won't be a pastor very long!

Be steadfast!

In ***Job 11:14*** he tells us, ***"If iniquity be in thine hand, put it far away, and let not wickedness dwell in thy tabernacles."*** Job tells us to put away evil and wickedness from our reach. He then goes on to say that we are not to let it dwell in our tabernacles, our church. He doesn't say not to let it in, because someone will bring it in with them. We are not to let it stay here! Job goes on in ***Job 11:15*** to say, ***"For then shalt thou lift up thy face without spot; yea, thou shalt be stedfast, and shalt not fear:"***

- In *I Corinthians 15:58* Paul says, *"Therefore, my beloved brethren, be ye stedfast, unmoveable, always abounding in the work of the Lord, forasmuch as ye know that your labour is not in vain in the Lord."*
- *Galatians 5:1, "Stand fast therefore in the liberty wherewith Christ hath made us free, and be not entangled again with the yoke of bondage."*
- *Ph. 1:27, "Only let your conversation be as it becometh the gospel of Christ: that whether I come and see you, or else be absent, I*

may hear of your affairs, that ye stand fast in one spirit, with one mind striving together for the faith of the gospel;"

Conclusion

We now know how to recognize the unstable/double minded person, we've heard the warnings against it, and we now know how to be steadfast.

Myths about Mega Churches

One can easily see the many fears that can be associated with the mega-church. But are such fears justified? Surprisingly, there are several myths concerning mega-churches. The first myth is that mega-churches are a uniquely American phenomenon. Mega-churches are not a uniquely American phenomenon. The reality is there are far more mega-churches outside of the United States than there are inside of the United States. The fact is all of the largest churches in the world are outside of America. For example, the church pastured by William Kumuyi in Lagos, Nigeria, has 120,000 in attendance. Ten of the eleven largest churches in the world are in Seoul, Korea. The largest Baptist church, the largest Methodist church, the largest Presbyterian Church, and the largest Pentecostal church are all in Seoul, Korea. The largest church in the world, Central Church, located on Yoido Island, in Seoul, Korea, has a half a million members. They have 50,000 home small groups. So this is not a phenomenon of America. In America, a mega-church is really tiny in comparison.

Another myth is that mega-churches attract people because of their size. Nobody goes to a church because of its size. Actually, the larger a church gets, the more headaches there are, and the more hassles you have to put up with, the further you have to walk to get to the service. Try to imagine the complexities of checking your children in and out of Sunday school that has an attendance of 5000 members. Such a school would almost necessitate a computerized system to ensure that the correct child is checked in and out by the correct parent. Add to this the additional problems with baby bottles and diaper bags and you can see that being "mega" also brings "mega difficulties".

The truth is the only people who like large churches are pastors. And they like them because they like to speak to big crowds (and of course the associated big collection plates). But people put up with the size in order to get the benefits – they say, "I like the teaching, I like the programs, I like the music, and I like the ministries," and things like that, not because of its size.

Actually there are two kinds of mega-churches. They just don't grow the same way. Some grow by transferred growth and some grow by conversion. Anytime you see a mega-church that grows instantly, as if it just explodes, and all of a sudden they go from zero to 5,000, that's a church that's growing by transfer growth. This means they've just become the hot act in town and everybody goes, "Let's just all go over there. That's the place to go so we'll all go."

They are known as "Church Hoppers." They hop from church to church. As a result the new church will grow in membership but at the expense of the former church. Jesus said, *"I'll make you fishers of men"*

(Matthew 4:19). What is meant here is that as the fish is drawn to the bait, the unsaved will be drawn to the Word of God through His Son Jesus Christ. Growth by conversion is the ideal method. This is how the first church grew in attendance (***Acts 2:41, 47***).

Is membership a requirement? Does one *have to* belong to a church? The answers to these and other similar questions will be covered in Chapter 7.

Chapter Seven

Church Membership: Required or Optional?

Many people do not see membership or participation in the church as very important. Some say, "The church cannot save you. Christ saves you. We need 'Christianity', not 'Churchianity.'" That is true, but what is usually *meant* by people who say this is that one can please God and be saved without being a member of the church. The question is: Will Christ save people outside the church? Others say, "I'm a good moral person. I believe in God and treat my family and neighbors right. Why do I need church membership?"

Many young people especially have rejected "organized religion." They may claim to accept Jesus, but want nothing to do with the church. Even some church members say, "We should preach Christ, not the church." They think we should teach unsaved people about forgiveness and salvation, but that we should not teach about the church until after they are saved. It might drive people away. Other members show by their lack of attendance and involvement that they don't consider church participation to be essential.

In the universal Church, the Body of Christ (***Romans 12:5***) is composed of all true believers in Jesus Christ; yet there is nothing in the Bible about "membership" in a local church assembly. As believers, we have our names written in the Lamb's book of life (***Revelations. 20:12***), which is the only "membership roll" spoken of in Scripture.

The New Testament churches apparently had no need of formal membership, relying instead on God to gather together believers into a local body.

- *"And the Lord added to them day by day those that were being saved" (Acts 2:47).*

This verse indicates that salvation was a prerequisite for being "added" to the church. Churches today that require salvation before membership are simply following the biblical model (***II Corinthians 6:14-18***.) Although there is no scriptural mandate for it, there is certainly nothing to prohibit it. Church membership is a way of officially identifying oneself with a local body of believers.

Church membership is a statement that a Christian is in agreement with that local church and is willing to be identified as a representative of it. Church membership is also valuable for organizational purposes and a good way of determining who is allowed to vote on important church decisions and/or who is involved in official church positions and functions. Church membership is not required of Christians. It is simply a way of saying, "I am a Christian and I believe _____(fill in the blank)_____ church is a good church."

How membership is abused

The typical church membership roll includes names of persons who may have left the congregation years ago and are presently attending another church or no church at all. Once a person has been baptized into a local church of a particular denomination, he generally remains a Baptist, Methodist, Presbyterian, etc., regardless of whether he ever attends church again. To help mitigate the embarrassment and to avoid the difficulties entailed in proper biblical oversight, modern churchmen devised the idea of an *inactive roll*. This improvisation further diminished the value of a church roll by constituting the legitimate status of "inactive Christian," one who is supposedly beyond the scope of church discipline.

A Church Full of Babies

I Corinthians 13:11

Introduction

An erroneous assumption is oftentimes made by many of us is that as we grow up physically we will mature as well. I don't know where we've come up with this mistaken idea. I've made decisions as an adult that showed my lack of maturity. I know many folks who are 40, 50, 60 years old and older who are still living like kids, behaving like children, and have never grown up. Many of us need to act our age instead of our shoe size.

There are four signs of a 'spiritual infant' according to the author: First, they were sluggish with regard to hearing (*I Corinthians 13:11*). There is an amazing similarity in the Greek, Hebrews and Chinese vocabulary – "to hear" and "to obey" are the same word. The author said in *5:11 "We have much to say about this, but it is hard to explain because you are slow to learn".* Literally, the term "to learn" means sluggish with regard to hearing (God's words).

DeSilva in his commentary on Hebrews says it is "not merely of nodding off during his sermon, but failing to respond honorably and wisely to the message of God. Not giving that message its due attention with all diligence".

Second, they ought to be teachers (*I Corinthians 13:12*). We may not be all bible study teachers or Sunday school teachers. But we are all teachers in the sense that we should demonstrate our faith and our conviction to those around us through our deeds and our words. He does not mean that they ought all to become public teachers, or preachers of the gospel, but that they ought to be able to explain to others the truths of the Christian religion. As parents they ought to be able to explain them to their children; as neighbors, to their neighbors; or as friends, to those who were inquiring the way to life.

To be teachers can also be a blessing. It means a community of individual members reinforcing (and supporting, and challenging) one another's hold on the minority culture's value and goals. However, instead of teaching others, they still needed to go through the elementary teaching (the milk diet) again.

Third, they were unskillful (inexperienced) in the word of righteousness (*v13*). Some commentators understand this as a technical term and associate "word of righteousness" with martyrdom (Polycarp – letter to the Philippians). It is a term associated with discipleship. In other words, the author is telling his audience, they are unskilled and uncommitted to the call of being a disciple of Jesus Christ.
Some examples:
- "When praises go up, blessings come down."
- Not in the Bible. "United we stand, divided we fall." NIB.
- "Every generation grows weaker but wiser." (***Prov 27:24***).
- NIB. "No cross no crown." NIB.
- "There is a time for all things." (***Eccl. 3:1***). NIB.
- "Come as you are." ***Matt 11:28, "Come unto me, all ye that labour and are heavy laden, and I will give you rest."***

Fourth, they lacked discerning power *(v14)*. They couldn't tell right from wrong, good from evil. Similarly, the spirit of discernment is especially important in the modern society, there are many grey areas in our lives, in our society. We need the spirit of discernment to guide us.

The author of Hebrews challenges baby-like believers to move from milk to solid food. After church, we'll have lunch—for most of us, this means grown-up food—not Gerbers! Milk is for beginners; solid food is for the mature. In the Christian life, after 'awhile' we should move beyond the basics and get into the 'meat' of God's word. We're no longer learning the foundational ABC's of God's revelation; we've progressed beyond that. But regrettably, some believers who by now ought to be teaching others still need instruction; they're stuck in spiritual infancy. They're inexperienced in applying God's truth to their lives--so much so that they're in need of having someone sit down with them and go over the basics again.

Here's my point: Are we growing, or are we still baby believers? Our church's mission statement indicates that we take spiritual growth seriously: ***"We proclaim Christ, counseling and instructing all people with all wisdom, so that we may present everyone complete (mature) in Him" (Colossians1:28).***

According to the author of Hebrews, we ought to be training others; this could mean teaching a Sunday School class or leading a small group Bible study, or by mentoring someone who's new to the faith. Some parents rely on Sunday school because they're not equipped to teach their children, and they struggle to answer their kids' questions about God. We can only lead people as far as we are ourselves.

In ***II Corinthians*** we see what's supposed to occur after initial trust in Jesus***: "If anyone is in Christ, they are a new creation; the old life is passing away, and all things are becoming new" (II Corinthians 5:17)***; this process of growth is supervised by the Holy Spirit. But it's a cooperative effort; we can stunt our own growth if we don't do our part. Plenty of spiritual food is available, but God's not about to force-feed us.

The last verse of ***Hebrews 5*** says that mature believers "train themselves." This is sports language, an athletic term referring to physical exercise at a gym. Some sluggish and unskilled believers are in dire need of a spiritual workout!

The offspring of these first century sluggards are filling our churches today. They come in to be entertained, to look for a "feel good" sermon, to be told how "good" we really are deep down inside, but there is no desire to face the truth of who we are, of the deeper teachings of Jesus, or to apply what they've learned through the study of God's Word. They are willing to come to church - now and then, but don't you dare ask them for any more than that; or you will catch their wrath and hear about how busy they are. They don't have time for Sunday night prayer or Bible study during the week, but they will change their schedule in a minute to go and watch their favorite team, they cannot catch a ride to church, but they can get a ride to the casino.

The problem is not that we are unable to learn. The problem is that we are unwilling to learn! We are sluggish when it comes to the things of God. We are lazy when it comes to the things of God. We are not willing to push on, to be stretched by God, to submit ourselves to the discipline necessary to understand God's Word and God's will.

The Hebrews were not the only ones addressed in the Bible who were slow to learn and lethargic concerning the thing of God. Let me give you a few examples.

- *I Corinthians 3:1-4, "And I, brethren, could not speak unto you as unto spiritual, but as unto carnal, even as unto babes in Christ. I have fed you with milk, and not with meat: for hitherto ye were not able to bear it, neither yet now are ye able. For ye are yet carnal: for whereas there is among you envying, and strife, and divisions, are ye not carnal, and walk as men? For while one saith, I am of Paul; and another, I am of Apollos; are ye not carnal?"*

When we look around our so-called "Christian" nation we do not see that the lives of the followers of Jesus are that much different than nonbelievers. I was reading George Barna's research on the Internet this past week and discovered some unsettling facts. Let me give you some examples: George Barna reports,

- Born again adults are more likely to experience a divorce than are non-born again adults (27% vs. 24%).
- Desiring to have a close, personal relationship with God ranks just sixth among the 21 life goals tested, trailing such desires as "living a comfortable lifestyle."
- Born again Christians spend seven times as much time on entertainment as they do on spiritual activities.
- Although two-thirds of all teenagers say they know all the basic teachings and principles of the Christian faith, two-thirds of them reject the existence of Satan, three-fifths reject the existence of

the Holy Spirit, and half believe that Jesus sinned during His lifetime.

- In a representative nationwide survey among born again adults, none of the individuals interviewed said that the single, most important goal in their life is to be a committed follower of Jesus Christ.

THE DANGERS OF SPIRITUAL IMMATURITY

FAITH EROSION

- *Hebrews 6:4-6, "For it is impossible for those who were once enlightened, and have tasted of the heavenly gift, and were made partakers of the Holy Ghost, And have tasted the good word of God, and the powers of the world to come, If they shall fall away, to renew them again unto repentance; seeing they crucify to themselves the Son of God afresh, and put him to an open shame."*

When it comes to spiritual maturity, you're either growing up or giving up. There is no in between. There's no standing still. You're either going forward or backward.

When we refuse to submit some area of our lives over to God spiritual transformation halts and gradual erosion begins. We can reach the point where we never perceive sin anymore and so we won't turn to God and ask his forgiveness.

If you've ever tried to break in a pair of shoes you'll understand how this works. I had a pair of running shoes that were a bit painful after the first mile. They rubbed blisters on my feet. If I ignored the discomfort the next time eventually callous built up. The skin thickened and I was no longer able to feel the pain in those spots.

This is what happens spiritually if we fail to submit an area of life to God. At first we feel the pain and discomfort of it. But, if we resist long enough, gradually the spiritual callous forms and we no longer even feel it. We never repent because we no longer believe that we've sinned. The Bible refers to this as a "reprobated mind".

It is time for us to move, spiritually, beyond the equivalent of "See Jack run. Run Jack run." It is time for us to grow up and to share what God is teaching us.

Why grow up?

Because we are told in *II Tim 2:15,* *"Study to shew thyself approved unto God, a workman that needeth not to be ashamed, rightly dividing the word of truth."*

14 "But solid food is for the mature, who by constant use have trained themselves to distinguish good from evil". The key to the verse is found in the phrase, *"who by constant use have trained themselves to distinguish good from evil."*

There are two important words to help us clarify what is meant here. The first word is translated **"use."** These folks through constant use have trained themselves to distinguish between good and evil. The word, "e[xij" (hexis) means, "a repeated activity, practice, doing again and again, doing repeatedly." If we do something over and over again we are going to get better at it. There is a lot of truth in the old adage, "Practice makes perfect." If we choose to surrender our hearts every morning to God's purposes and will, then we will see more of Christ shine through us, we will see His Word begin to shape our lives, and we will begin to make decisions that better represent His character.

The second word that we should understand is the word translated **"trained."** The Greek work, "gumna,zw" (gumnazo) means, "exercise, train in gymnastic discipline, mental and spiritual training and discipline."

Studying God's Word, spending time in prayer, and seeking to know the heart of God is not always fun. I can show you fun if you want fun. Let's watch a movie, chill in front of the tube, go catch a good game, hanging out at the club on a Friday night, or take a vacation. Now that's fun! But for those who have a higher aim in life, for those who want to know the Lord in an intimate way, and allow Him to shape and guide their lives then it means that we say "No" to what our flesh cries out for and "Yes" to what our spirit is craving.

Conclusion

Today, God is calling us to grow up. When will we put away the childish things of this world and seek the things of God? If God is speaking to your heart and stirring a hunger in you to go beyond the ABC's of faith; then I want to invite you to invite Jesus into your heart as Lord and Savior of your life.

Dear friends, even though we are talking like this, we really don't believe that it applies to you. We are confident that you are meant for better things, things that come with salvation. For God is not unfair. He will not forget how hard you have worked for him and how you have shown your love for him by caring for other Christians, as you still do. ***Heb. 6:9-10 (NLT)*** We're not alone in this pursuit. God is actively watching and working with us. He wants us to be spiritually mature.

Someone may say, "I'm not a member of any church. Is it not then the case that no church has the rule over *me*? This Scripture cannot apply to me." ***Hebrews 13:17*** assumes what *should* be the case for every Christian; it presents the norm for the Christian life. Would not every true child of God who understood the implications of this verse *want* to put himself in the place where it was possible for him to obey this plain apostolic command? It must be remembered that a person is blessed to the degree that he obeys (***Psalms.119:2***).

Many Christians cringe at the idea of church authorities having rule over them. After all, wasn't our nation forged out of the wilderness by self-reliant, self-made men? Some of that early "rugged individualism" has permeated into our psyches, and consequently we do not take well to the idea of submission to authority (again I remind you of Mississippi having the largest number of churches per capita). We like to think that we have gotten to where we are in life by our own power and we really do not need to submit. But submission is a biblical concept. We must obey them that have the rule over us in order to be in submission to Christ.

The Bible commands, ***"Obey them that have the rule over you, and submit yourselves (Hebrews 13:18)."*** This does not mean to obey in some vague way, simply giving lip service. One cannot obey those empowered to rule in Christ's church if he never joins. One simply cannot submit to the church's lawfully-constituted leadership unless one becomes a member. One could never be *excommunicated* if he had never been a *communicant* member to begin with. The Lord's Supper is a fellowship meal only to be given to faithful saints who have properly submitted themselves to church membership, for it is required that all things be done decently and in order (*I Corinthians 14:40*).

Since the church itself is held in such low regard today, little wonder church membership is not highly regarded. Many civic organizations or professional associations have much higher requirements for membership than the church. In how many local civic clubs could one remain a member in good standing while never attending or paying dues?

The very fact that civic organizations should have higher standards of membership than the church of Jesus Christ is truly a shame. For no other organization has the power of the keys, the power to admit people into heaven or ban them from the presence of God.

Is church membership, then, a necessity, or is it somehow optional ("I can join if I feel like it")? Let's put it another way: Is obedience to Christ a necessity or an option? This question must be asked today because many people have the mistaken idea that to be a Christian, all they must do is pray a simple prayer and then they will be forever saved. No particular transformation may ever be evident in their lives. They may never be able to give up any pet sins. They may never have any desire to read their Bible or attend church regularly. They may never exercise spiritual leadership in their family or have a credible Christian witness. They may never amount to anything for Christ. But that's all right (they believe) for there are two levels of sanctification: Christian and Super-Christian! Not all Christians must become obedient to Christ. Not all must deal with sin. Not all must read their Bible or attend church regularly. Those things are only for Super Christians, those who have attained a higher level of spirituality.

Is this what Scripture teaches? Not at all! The Apostle John wrote, **"If we say that we have fellowship with him, and walk in darkness, we lie, and do not the truth.... He that saith, I know him, and keepeth not his commandments, is a liar, and the truth is not in him" (I John 1:6, 2:4).**

Thus, the Scriptures know nothing of a Christian who will not give up his sin, who will not keep God's commandments. Those who refuse to bring their lives into conformity with the will of God place themselves in mortal danger of eternal damnation.

Is church membership optional? For the Christian, who is obligated to live his life according to every word that proceeds out of the mouth of God, it is only necessary to determine: Does God's Word require it or not? What does our text say? "Obey them that have the rule over you, and submit yourselves." That is pretty clear, isn't it? There is no getting around the fact that the disciple of Jesus Christ is under solemn obligation to submit obediently to the lawful authority of Christ's church. Submission to lawful authority, whether familial, civil, or ecclesiastical, is not a popular concept these days, but it is what God requires in the interest of a well-ordered and prosperous society, and the church must begin to preach this doctrine again or face God's righteous fury.

The inability to follow leadership and the differences in doctrine has led to the different denominations that exist in the church today. What is a denomination? How did it start? This is explored in Chapter 8.

Chapter Eight

Denominations

Introduction

If you were to type the word "church denominations" into your internet search engine you will get back over 210,000 "hits". Why so many? If we all serve the same God, believe in His only begotten Son, and have been filled with His Holy Ghost, then why so many denominations? Just what is a denomination? A **denomination**, in the Christian sense of the word, is an identifiable religious body under a common name, structure, and/or doctrine.

Christianity is composed of, but not limited to, five major branches of Churches: Roman Catholic, Eastern Orthodox, Oriental Orthodox, Anglican and Protestant. Each of these five branches has important subdivisions. Because the Protestant subdivisions do not maintain a common theology or earthly leadership, they are far more distinct than the subdivisions of the other four groupings. **Denomination** typically refers to one of the many Christian groupings including each of the multitudes of Protestant subdivisions.

Denominationalism is an ideology which views some or all Christian groups as being, in some sense, versions of the same thing regardless of their distinguishing labels. The history of church denominations begins with the earliest movements and reforms within the early church.

History of Denominations

For the first thousand years of Christian history, there were no "denominations" within the Christian church as there are today. Various offshoot groups certainly existed, but they were considered "heresies" and not part of the Christian church. Most were small and, until the 16th century, were never very influential. From the beginnings of Christianity through the Middle Ages, there was only one - the Catholic ("universal") church. Basically, if one did not belong to the Church, he was not considered a Christian.

The first division within Christendom came in 1054 with the **"Great Schism"** between the Western Church and the Eastern Church. From that point forward, there were two large branches of Christianity, which came to be known as the Catholic Church (in the West) and the Orthodox Church (in the East).

The next major division occurred in the 16th century with the **Protestant Reformation**. The Reformation was famously sparked when Martin Luther posted his *95 Theses* in 1517, but "Protestantism" as a movement officially began in 1529. The Reformation was a movement that was designed to "reform" the Catholic Church and instead led to the breakup of Christianity as it once was.

The major issues that Martin Luther and others opposed was the Catholic Church's beliefs and practices that included purgatory, particular judgment, devotion to Mary, the intercession of the saints, most of the sacraments, and the authority of the Pope.

1517 also marked the publication of the *Protestation*, directed at the imperial government. The authors, German princes who wanted the freedom to choose the faith of their territory, protested that "in matters which concern God's honor and salvation and the eternal life of our souls, everyone must stand and give account before God for himself."[11]
With its emphasis on individual interpretation of scripture and a measure of religious freedom, the Reformation marked not only a break between Protestantism and Catholicism, but the beginning of denominationalism as we know it today. This historical perspective is perhaps the best way to make sense of the initially astounding variety of Christian denominations.

Those who remained within the fold of Roman Catholicism argued that central regulation of doctrine is necessary to prevent confusion and division within the church and corruption of its beliefs. Those who broke from the church, on the other hand, insisted that it was precisely this policy of control that had already led to corruption of the true faith. They demanded that believers be allowed to read the Scriptures for themselves and act in accordance with their consciences. This issue of religious authority continues to be a fundamental difference in perspective between Catholic and Orthodox Christians on one hand, and Protestant Christians on the other.

Gnosticism infiltrated the early church and showed itself in many forms. This belief system eliminated the historic foundations of Christianity. It did not acknowledge God as the God of the Old Testament. Jesus had no real human body, death, or resurrection. He was an enlightened being who brought salvation for the few who were capable of enlightenment.

There were some movements considered heresies by the early church which do not exist today and are not generally referred to as denominations. Examples include the Gnostics (who had believed in an esoteric dualism), the Ebionites (who denied the divinity of Jesus), and the Arians. The greatest divisions in Christianity today, however, are between Eastern Orthodoxy, Roman Catholicism, and various denominations formed during and after the Protestant Reformation. The churches most commonly associated with Protestantism can be divided into four groups:

- **Mainline Protestants** - a North American phrase - are those who trace their lineage to Luther, Calvin, or Anglicanism. The doctrines of the Reformation are their doctrines. They include such denominations as Lutherans, Presbyterians, and Methodists.
- **Anabaptists** are a movement that developed from the Radical Reformation. Today, denominations such as Baptists, Pentecostals, Brethren, Mennonites and Amish eschew infant baptism and see baptism as aligned with a demonstration of the gifts of the spirit.
- **Non-Trinitarian** movements reject the doctrine of the trinity. Today, they include such denominations as the Universalists, Unitarians, and some Quakers.
- **Restorationists** are a more recent movement. Today, they include such denominations as the Latter-day Saints (Mormons), and Adventists.[12]

The majority of Christians never embraced these early movements. The church remained faithful to historic Christianity. By the latter third of the second century, the church was known as the "Catholic" Church. Ignatius, referring to the church as universal rather than local, first used this term. It became strongly consolidated and united relatively independent congregations into one body. The person who could belong to the church was one who acknowledged the creed, the New Testament canon (scriptures) and the authority of the bishops as opposed to the requirements for membership.

Denominations of Today

Denominations today are many and varied. According to the World Christian Encyclopedia (year 2000 version), global Christianity had 33,820 denominations with 3,445,000 congregations/churches composed of 1,888 million affiliated Christians. Today that number has grown to over 41,000. The original "mainline" denominations mentioned above have spawned numerous offshoots such as Assemblies of God, Christian and Missionary Alliance, Nazarenes, Evangelical Free, independent Bible churches, and others. Some denominations emphasize slight doctrinal differences, but more often they simply offer different styles of worship to fit the differing tastes and preferences of Christians. But make no mistake: as believers, we must be of one mind on the essentials of the faith, but beyond that there is great deal of latitude in how Christians should worship in a corporate setting. This latitude is what causes so many different "flavors" of Christianity. A Presbyterian church in Uganda will have a style of worship much different from a

Presbyterian church in Colorado, but their doctrinal stand will be, for the most part, the same. Diversity is a good thing, but disunity is not. If two churches disagree doctrinally, debate and dialogue over the Word may be called for. This type of "iron sharpening iron" (**Proverbs 27:17**) is beneficial to all. If they disagree on style and form, however, it is fine for them to remain separate. This separation, though, does not lift the responsibility Christians have to love one another (**I John 4:11-12**) and ultimately be united as one in Christ (**John 17:21-22**).

Included in this list are all of the major religious groups in the U.S. that consider themselves to be Christian. It is important to realize that many individuals, particularly conservative Christians, reject many of these groups as sub-Christian, quasi-Christian or non-Christian, because they hold beliefs that deviate from historic Christianity.

Denominational membership numbers are difficult to compare exactly, because many faith groups have different definitions of church membership. Some groups:

- Do not publish numbers. This includes Christian Scientists;
- Count only currently active members
- Include everyone who was baptized, usually as an infant, whether they actually darkened the door of a church later in life. This includes the roman Catholic Church
- Exaggerate their numbers in order to appear like a larger group.

U.S. membership numbers, as supplied by various denominations (in thousands) are: [11]

Denomination	Membership, in Thousands `2004	Membership, in Thousands `1996	Comments
Adventist Church	927	808	
Apostolic Christian Church	18	4	Nazarene
Apostolic Christian Churches of America	13	11	
Baptist Churches	30002	36613	
Brethren	191	51	German Baptist
Christian Brethren	95		Plymouth Brethren
Christian Church	805	938	Disciples of Christ
Christian Congregation	119	112	
Christian and Missionary Alliance	382	302	
Christian Union, *Churches of Christ in*	10	10	
Churches of Christ	1500	1651	
Churches of God	287	257	
Church of the Nazarene	637	598	
Community Churches, *Inter Council of*	117	500	
Congregational Christian churches	65	90	
Conservative Congregational Christian Conference	41	37	
Eastern Orthodox Churches	4218	5302	
Episcopal Church	2333	2505	
Evangelical Church	12	12	
Evangelical Congregational Church	21	24	
Evangelical Covenant Church	101	90	
Evangelical Free Church of America	243	227	
Grace Gospel Fellowship	60	60	

Independent Fundamental Churches of America	62	70	
Jehovah Witnesses	989	946	
Latter – Day Saints	5448	4766	Mormon
Liberal Catholic Church	7	3	
Lutheran Churches	8152	8350	
Mennonite Churches	346	294	Includes Old Order Amish
Methodist Churches	12266	13533	
Metropolitan Community Churches	44	30	
Missionary Church	41	28	
Moravian Churches	26	52	
National Organization of the New Apostolic Church	36	42	
National Spiritist Association of Church		4	
Pentecostal Churches	11362	10606	
Polish National Catholic Church		150	
Presbyterian Churches	4048	4193	
Reformed Churches	1748	2039	
Reformed Episcopal Church	6	7	
Roman Catholic Church	65260	60191	
Salvation Army	455	443	
Schwenkfelder Church		3	
Society of Friends	206	108	
Swedenborgian Church		2	
United Brethren in Christ		25	

* a.k.a. Quakers

The Downside of Christian Denominations

There seems to be at least two major problems with denominationalism. First, nowhere in Scripture is there a mandate for denominationalism; to the contrary the mandate is for union and connectivity. Thus, the second problem is that history tells us that denominationalism is the result of, or caused by, conflict and confrontation which leads to division and separation. Jesus told us that a house divided against itself cannot stand. This general principle can and should be applied to the church.

We find an example of this in the Corinthian church which was struggling with issues of division and separation. There were those who thought that they should follow Paul and those who thought they should follow the teaching of Apollos, *I Corinthians 1:12, "What I am saying is this: each of you says, "I'm with Paul," or "I'm with Apollos," or "I'm with Cephas," or "I'm with Christ."*

This alone should tell you what Paul thought of denominations or anything else that separates and divides the body. But let's look further; in *I Corinthians 1:13*, Paul asks very pointed questions, *"Is Christ divided? Was it Paul who was crucified for you? Or were you baptized in Paul's name?"*

This makes clear how Paul feels, he (Paul) is not the Christ, he is not the one crucified and his message has never been one that divides the church or would lead someone to worship Paul instead of Christ. Obviously, according to Paul, there is only one church and one body of believers and anything that is different weakens and destroys the church. He makes this point stronger in *I Corinthians 3:4* by saying that anyone who says they are of Paul or of Apollos is carnal.

Here are some of the problems we are faced with today as we look at denominationalism and its more recent history:
- Denominations are based on disagreements over the interpretation of Scripture. An example would be the meaning

and purpose of baptism. Is baptism a requirement for salvation or is it symbolic of the salvation process? There are denominations on both sides of this issue and have used the issue to separate and form denominations.
- Disagreements over the interpretation of Scripture are taken personally and become points of contention. This leads to arguments which can and have done much to destroy the witness of church.
- The church should be able to resolves its differences inside the body; but once again history tells us that this doesn't happen. Today the media uses our differences against us to demonstrate that we are not unified in thought or purpose.
- Denominations are used by man out of self-interest. There are denominations today that are in a state of self-destruction as they are being led into apostasy by those who are promoting their personal agendas.
- The value of unity is found in the ability to pool our gifts and resources to promote the Kingdom to a lost world. This runs contrary to divisions caused by denominationalism.

What is a believer to do? Should we ignore denominations, should we just not go to church and worship on our own at home? The answer to both questions is no. What we should be seeking is a body of believers where the Gospel of Christ is preached, where you as an individual can have a personal relationship with the Lord, where you can join in Biblical ministries that are spreading the Gospel and glorifying

God. Church is important and all believers need to belong to a body that fits the above criteria. We need relationships that can only be found in the body of believers, we need the support that only the church can offer, and we need to serve God in the community as well as individually.

Pick a church on the basis of its relationship to Christ, how well it is serving the community. Pick a church where the pastor is preaching the Gospel without fear and is encouraged to do so. Christ and His church is all about your relationship to Him and to each other. As believers, there are certain basic doctrines that we must believe, but beyond that there is latitude on how we can serve and worship; it is this latitude that is the only good reason for denominations. This is diversity and not disunity. The first allows us to be individuals in Christ, the latter divides and destroys.

If the concept of denominations weren't enough to confuse believers there are now new terms which they must face. They are "evangelicals" and "millennials".

Evangelicals

The term "Evangelical" gained national interest during the 2008 Presidential election. Since then both Democrats and Republicans have reached out to this suddenly relevant voting force…but who are they?

What is an Evangelical?
According to the National Associations of Evangelicals, Evangelicals take the Bible seriously and believe in Jesus Christ as Savior and Lord. The term "Evangelical" comes from the Greek word

euangelion, meaning "the good news" or the "gospel." Thurs, the evangelical faith focuses on the "good news" of salvation brought to sinners by Jesus Christ. Evangelicals re a vibrant and diverse group, including believers found in many churches, denominationsa and nations. They bring together Reformed, Holiness, Anabaptist, Pentecostal, Charismatic and other traditions. The core theological convictions of evangelicals provide unity in the midst of our diversity. The NAE statement of Faith offers a standard of these evangelical convictions. Historian David Bebbington also provides a hel0pful summary of evangelical distinctives, identifying four primary characteristics of evangelicalism:

- Conversionism: The belief that lives need to be transformed through a "born again" experience and a lifelong process of following Jesus.
- Activism: The expression and demonstration of the gospel in missionary and social reform efforts
- Biblicism: A high regard for and obedience to the Bible as the ultimate authority
- Crucicentrism: A stress on the sacrifice of Jesus Christ on the cross as making possible the redemption of humanity.

These distinctive and theological convictions define us, not political, social, or cultural trends. In fact, many evangelicals rarely use the term "evangelical" to describe themselves, focusing simply on the core convictions of the triune God, the Bible, faith, Jesus, salvations, evangelism, and discipleship[13].

Millennials

What is a Millennial?

The Millennial generation is a group of young people whose birth years range from 1980 to 2000. This generation is actually just slightly larger than the Baby Boom generation (born from 1946 to 1964). Nearly 78 million Millennials were born between 1980 and 2000.

Millennials ware already having an impact on business, the workplace, churches, and other organizations. They certainly are having an impact on politics. The 18 to 29 year old Millennials voted for Barack Obama in 2008 by a significant margin. Because of their impact in business, politics, and the church, they are simply too large and too influential to ignore.

Millennials and Religion

The Millennial generation is the least religious generation in American history. They are likely to have a syncretistic belief system. In other words, he or she will take portions of belief from various faiths and non-faiths and blend them together in to a unique spiritual system.

In their book, *"The Millennials: Connecting to America's Largest Generation,"*[14] Thom and Jess Rainer found that this generation is less likely to care about religion or spiritual matters than previous generations. When they were asked in an open-ended questions what was important to them, 0piritual matters were sixth on the list. Preceding them in importance were family, friends, education, career, and spouse/partner.

When asked to describe themselves, two-thirds (65 percent) used the term Christian. Interestingly, nearly three in ten (28 percent) picked either atheism, agnosticism, or no preference. In other words, they have moved completely away from certain belief in God.

When asked if they were "born-again Christians", using a precise definition provided by the interviewers, only 20 percent affirmed this definition of belief and experience. And when presented with seven statements about orthodox Christian belief, the researchers found that only 6 percent of Millennials could affirm them and thus could be properly defined as Evangelical. {1}

A third (34 percent) of Millennials said that no one can know what will happen when they die. But more than one-fourth (26 percent) said they believe they will go to heaven when they die because they have accepted Christ as their Savior. {2}

Church attendance has been decreasing with each generation. The Millennial generation illustrates that trend. Nearly two-thirds (65 percent) rarely or never attend religious services. {3} About one-fourth (24 percent) are active in church (meaning they attend at least once a week). This might suggest that a number of Millennials who attend church do so as seekers. In other words, they are at least spiritually interested enough to visit a church even though they may not be saved.

The Millennial generation presents a significant challenge for us as Christians. The largest and least religious generation in American history is here and making an impact. If the church and Christian organizations are to be vibrant and effective in the 21st Century, pastors and Christian leaders need to know how to connect to the Millennials.

The first step is to understand them and their beliefs.

Religion based on Tradition

Matthew 15:1-14

Introduction

There is often disparity between how things are and how they should be. That reminds me of the story of a tiny but dignified old lady who was at an art gallery looking at an exhibition of modern art. Viewing one particular painting, she asked, "What on earth is that?" The artist was standing nearby and he smiled condescendingly. "That, my dear lady, is supposed to be a mother and her child." "Well, then," snapped the little old lady, "Why isn't it?"

In the previous chapter, Jesus and Peter walked on water. Jesus' fame is spreading. People are gathering to merely touch the hem of His garment and are healed. This disturbs the religious leaders and they are irate. They confront Jesus hoping to discredit Him.

SOURCE OF DISAGREEMENT
Matthew 15:1-2

You can get into a lot of trouble with people when you violate their customs. The Scribes and Pharisees were trying to condemn Jesus and His followers because of traditions. They had taken something simple and made a doctrine out of it. How many of you think that you can manage to wash your hands without a detailed description? They had an elaborate ritual: Free hands of dirt, point fingers up while water was poured over them allowing water to run off the wrist. Rub each hand with the other fist. If a second washing was necessary, there was a ritual, too. In their opinion, to neglect the ritual washing before eating food was like the sin of adultery. In this way, they substituted mere outward cleansing for the inner cleanness that God sought. It is certainly a good idea to wash your hands, but that won't get you to heaven.

In *v9* Jesus says, **"But in vain they do worship me, teaching for doctrines the commandments of men."** Commandments of men, traditions of elders.... people's opinions elevated to the level of truth.

We should follow the example of the ***Thessalonians***
- ***(1 Thess 2:13) "When ye received the word of God which ye heard of us, ye received it not as the word of men, but as it is in truth, the word of God."***

We may have thoughts and opinions, but we can never hold those above the revealed Word of God. If we begin to elevate our preferences and opinions above the truth of Scripture, we are just as guilty as the scribes and Pharisees. God's Word is sovereign and inerrant – It is divinely inspired and revealed and deserves our obedience.
- ***2 Timothy 3:16-17 says, "All scripture is given by inspiration of God, and is profitable for doctrine, for reproof, for correction, for instruction in righteousness: That the man of God may be perfect, throughly furnished unto all good works."***
- ***2 Peter 1:21 says, "For the prophecy came not in old time by the will of man: but holy men of God spake as they were moved by the Holy Ghost."***

SIDESTEPPING THE DIVINE
Matthew 15:3, 15:6

The religious leaders of Jesus' day were adamant about traditions but dodged the commands of God. Does that seem familiar? How frequent a practice that is today! Interpret Scripture in the light of modern culture. They spent their efforts in devising loopholes that justified their disobedience to God.

Jesus said that they transgressed or violated God's commands with their traditions. He gave an example of their contemporary practice that skirted the commands of God in not supporting or honoring their parents. They had invalidated God's commands with their traditions and superimposed the traditions over God's Word.

Today, if something isn't comfortable or politically correct, we set it aside and come up with alternatives. We may congratulate ourselves on our sophistication, but we still must be judged by God. We interpret scripture in view of modern standards on issues of marriage, morality, and the qualifications of a pastor.

There are many examples but consider one: Our society says, "All roads lead to God and every religion is just as good as any other religion." But *John 14:6 tells us, "Jesus saith, I am the way, the truth, and the life: no man cometh unto the Father, but by me."* Can both be right? *Acts 4:12 says, "Neither is there salvation in any other: for there is none other name under heaven given among men, whereby we must be saved."*
But as *Romans 3:4 state, "Let God be true, but every man a liar"*

SIGNFICANCE OF DECISION

Matthew 15:7, 15:11

Jesus declared these religious leaders to be hypocrites and blind leaders of the blind. He drew on the words of the prophet Isaiah and characterized their worship as insincere Lip service. We might say that it is full of hot air. It is just so much bluster, but God sees through it. Jesus announced that their worship was vain, empty, self-serving manipulation- Hollow and shallow. Could we be going through the motions but God not receive our worship? Is our worship self-serving and empty? Do our lips say and pray and sing that which does not harmonize with what is within our hearts?

Look at *Matthew 15:12*. The disciples were very much attuned to the fact that Jesus' pronouncement offended the Pharisees, but Jesus was not concerned with their tender sensitivity to the truth. Look at Jesus' response in *Matthew 15:13*. *"Rooted up".* Has God planted you? Have you by Faith accepted the message of Salvation? If you "plant" yourself in a church without a saving knowledge of Jesus, you may fool others, but God will sort it out. For this, consider Jesus' parable of the Wheat and Tares from *Matthew 13*. Especially revealing is *Matthew 13:41-42*.

In *Matthew 15:14* we see the tragic result of following vain religion. Following the wrong directives will cause catastrophe. Both fall into the ditch. Tragic outcome!

Conclusion

Don't make the mistake of following religion. Whether we have gained our beliefs from churches or family members, those beliefs that are not confirmed in the Bible will lead us astray. It is not a stringent adherence to beliefs that will save us. Only a relationship with Christ through repentance and faith can forgive our sin. We can't afford to follow anyone BUT JESUS.

Jesus said I am the way, the truth, and the life. Is He all that to you? He died so that you might live. He rose on the third day justified so that you can have victory over death just like Him. He's sitting on the right hand of God the Father right now interceding for us. One day He's coming back…will you be ready? Whosoever will let him come! God bless you!

Is YOUR religion in vain?
James 1:26, 27

Introduction

Have you ever been deceived? Has anyone ever pretended to be someone they were not? Has someone told you they would do something when they had no intention of doing so?

As pastor I have often felt deceived by persons making vows and promises and within days or months forgetting their own words. By those who have made confession of faith, promising to live out Christian faith in worship and service. And when I confront them, they somehow don't understand what is bothering me. Perhaps my pride is hurt. I thought they were sincere. That what they said with their mouth and their outer worship of God came from a faith within them that was real. I may even have given my opinion that their faith was real to the church. Now I feel betrayed and even foolish. They stop coming to church, start living with someone, and live a life that does not care about what God says at all - so it seems to me. They pulled the wool over my eyes. I was deceived by them. Their profession of faith seems so false.

In the first chapter of James he uses the word deceived three times. But the deception he is talking about here is much more dangerous than being deceived by others. James warns us not to deceive ourselves. To think we are something we are not. He warns us not to be deceived into thinking we are believers or followers of Jesus Christ. Not to be deceived into thinking we are part of God's kingdom, that we have been regenerated or converted. That's scary.

We considered this when we looked at the *Sermon on the Mount*; to come before God, expecting His arms to be open to receive us. Instead he says **"Depart from me, I never knew you"**.

Is your faith sincere or will God say "I never knew you" to you?" Is your religion worthless or is it pure and faultless? James offers us three litmus tests to see if our faith is real. And as we look at these three tests, look at yourself and ask God to convict you if it is not.

We may like to pretend all is well but that does little good. Only when we know we are sick, do we take steps to get well. These three tests concern our religion. Our religion means our outer act of worship. We can stand before God and sing praise to Him, we can bow down before Him and we can raise our hands in worship. But is it worthless or is it pure and faultless? In other words is it real, or is it in vain?

What is important is that we are not just listeners, but doers. That the word of God has touched and changed our hearts in such a way that our lives are changed; that we become doers of the word. And the three tests before us each are concerned about doing.

Controlled

James 1:26

The first question or test involves Control: Do you keep a tight rein on your tongue?

As you read on through the book of James, he will talk more about the danger and the power of our tongues. It is so easy to quickly say things that we either should not or wish we had not have said.

There's a story of a young man who went horseback riding. He was told the importance of the rein. It controls the speed and direction the horse goes. Tighten it and it slows down. Loosen and shake it and the horse speeds up. Pull to side and the horse turns. It seemed very simple. After little while the young man felt more comfortable. He let the horse know he wanted him to speed up. But he wanted it to go from five to ten miles per hour. The horse thought he wanted 25 mph. And as the horse sped up the young man panicked, he felt out of control, and forgot to pull in the rein until someone nearby reminded him to pull in the rein. Such is the case with our tongues; they can easily run away from us.

We need to keep control of our tongue. Why? Because the tongue reveals what is really in side of us. The Pharisees worshiped God, they had religion. One day they complained that disciples didn't wash their hands before they ate. Jesus answered them, **Matthew 15:8-11 "'These people honor me with their lips, but their hearts are far from me. They worship me in vain; their teachings are but rules taught by men.'"** Jesus called the crowd to him and said, "Listen and understand. What goes into a man's mouth does not make him 'unclean,' but what comes out of his mouth, that is what makes him 'unclean.'"

What we say makes us unclean? Why? **Luke 6:45, " The good man brings good things out of the good stored up in his heart, and the** *evil man brings evil things out of the evil stored up in his heart. For out of the overflow of his heart, his mouth speaks."*

The problem is that our words reveal what is really in our heart. If we curse God's name, if we gossip, if we hurt others with our words, has our heart really been changed by the Holy Spirit. ***Mat 7:17-18,** "Likewise every good tree bears good fruit, but a bad tree bears bad fruit. A good tree cannot bear bad fruit, and a bad tree cannot bear good fruit."*

As Christians we all fail at times. Many want to say things we should not and sometimes we do. But are our tongues out of control. Or are they controlled by Holy Spirit? **Is your religion in vain?** Let's ask God to give us the power to control our tongues.

COMPASSION

James 1:27a

Let us consider the second test, it involves Compassion: are we compassionate? James says that the religion that our Father accepts as pure and faultless is this: to look after orphans and widows in their distress.

We are to look after - the Greek word for this is episkeptomai. Jesus used this word in *Matthew 25:36,*
- *"I needed clothes and you clothed me, I was sick and you looked after me, I was in prison and you came to visit me."*
- *Mat 25:43, "I was a stranger and you did not invite me in, I needed clothes and you did not clothe me, I was sick and in prison and you did not look after me."*

This word is translated as "visit" in the KJV - we are to visit the orphans and the widows. These words mean more than to simply make a social call. We are to visit them so that we may be aware of their needs and in order, to take care of their needs. In other words we are to be concerned about them and have compassion for them that moves us to action.

The reason why this compassion is a mark of true religion is that this compassion is something that reflects the heart of God. Throughout the Bible, God cares for the orphans and the widows. He cares about those in distress and tells us to care for them.

- And so, although James is talking about orphans and widows specifically, God calls us to care for all those in need: **Deuteromy 10:17-19, "17 *For the LORD your God is God of gods, and Lord of lords, a great God, a mighty, and a terrible, which regardeth not persons, nor taketh reward:18 He doth execute the judgment of the fatherless and widow, and loveth the stranger, in giving him food and raiment.19 Love ye therefore the stranger: for ye were strangers in the land of Egypt."***
- And this love is to be expressed in action" **Deuteronomy 14:27-29, "27 *And the Levite that is within thy gates; thou shalt not forsake him; for he hath no part nor inheritance with thee.28 At the end of three years thou shalt bring forth all the tithe of thine increase the same year, and shalt lay it up within thy gates:29 And the Levite, (because he hath no part nor inheritance with thee,) and the stranger, and the fatherless, and***

the widow, which are within thy gates, shall come, and shall eat and be satisfied; that the LORD thy God may bless thee in all the work of thine hand which thou doest."

And so James reminds the early Christians and he reminds us that we must continue to act in compassion. To all people but especially to other believers in need.

- ***Gal 6:10 Therefore, as we have opportunity, let us do good to all people, especially to those who belong to the family of believers.***

In our passage from *1 Timothy* we receive some specific instructions that show we must use discernment in looking after widows. And we should use discernment in all acts of compassion.

In regards to believing widows, Paul gives the following guidelines:
- No relatives
- At least 60 years old
- Lives a Christian life.

I don't believe these guidelines are guidelines to be following in each act of kindness since they have to do with those who are placed on the list of widows - those who receive regular, ongoing care. Not deal with single time of need, although we then also need to be wise. And so as we consider the specific guidelines for helping widows, we learn some principles as well.

If you are like me, I find it hard to deal with those in need. Sometimes I feel they are a bother and they use me. Then I might feel guilty. What is important is that I feel compassion towards them. But if

I have clear guidelines which I try to apply to situations, then I can make sure that I am acting responsible and not due to a lack of compassion.

Is your religion in vain? Oh, you pray, worship, study the word, teach - but do you look after those in distress? If not, is your faith genuine? CONTROLLED, COMPASSIONATE? Or is your religion in vain?

CLEAN

James 1:27b

The last and final test involves being CLEAN. James says that a mark of a true believer is that he keeps himself from being polluted by the world. The Greek here says that we are to be unspotted or without spot. We are to be unblemished with the ways or pollution of the world. By world it means the world's system, the world's ways of doing things.

- *1 John 2:16, "For all that is in the world, the lust of the flesh, and the lust of the eyes, and the pride of life, is not of the Father, but is of the world."*

So the world, according to John is the cravings of sinful man - our worldly desires, the lust of the eyes - false desires, and boasting - our ego or pride.

Paul refers to the following the wisdom, ways, and principles of this world:

- *1 Cor 1:20, "Where is the wise? where is the scribe? where is the disputer of this world? hath not God made foolish the wisdom of this world?"*

- *Col 2:8, "Beware lest any man spoil you through philosophy and vain deceit, after the tradition of men, after the rudiments of the world, and not after Christ."*
- *Jesus said Matt 6:24, "No man can serve two masters: for either he will hate the one, and love the other; or else he will hold to the one, and despise the other. Ye cannot serve God and mammon."*

The word for money is mammon or world good or profit. The world's ways becomes gods to us.

And so I ask you are you clean or polluted? The world pollutes us through television, music, books, radio. We are bombarded by worldly pollution - acid rain is the least of our problems. When I was young one would never hear a bad word on television. Now anything goes, and ungodly relationships are flaunted before our eyes...If we let it.

We need to look at what we are taking in. We need to look at ourselves and say - what is of God and what is of the world? We live in the world but we are not of this world. "Do I bring God's purity into the world or is it polluting me? Am I a light on a hill that all can see or has the pollution within me blocked the light of Christ?"

Paul tells us what to do.

- **Rom 12:2, *"And be not conformed to this world: but be ye transformed by the renewing of your mind, that ye may prove what is that good, and acceptable, and perfect, will of God."***

We have looked at the three marks of pure and faultless religion. Is your faith genuine? Read *James 1:26, 27*. We will all fail at times, we need to confess and ask God to cleanse us and purify us, through and through. But if we do not live according to these three marks, subject to some failures, is our faith real? Is your religion in vain?

Conclusion

Each day you wake up this week remember three words - CONTROLLED, COMPASSIONATE, CLEAN. Ask God to enable you to control your tongue, to be compassionate, and to be clean of the worlds' pollution. At end of day ask - "Was my tongue controlled? Was I compassionate? Was I clean?"

Jesus controlled His tongue. He became angry but He sinned not. He cried over the people when He saw their condition, He wept over the death of Lazarus; He was compassionate. When Satan tempted Him in the desert He did not yield to him, Jesus remained clean. He took all of our sins upon Himself and became our blood sacrifice and was acceptable to God. God raised Him on the third day and now He, Jesus, the Christ, our Deliverer, our Redeemer, sits on the right hand side of God the Father. One day He's coming back for His church that has remained Controlled, Compassionate, and Clean. Will you be in that church? Is your religion in vain? Glory to God!

Armed with knowledge of the history of the church, and after taking a closer look at the church of today, we can now take a look into the future and try to envision the church of tomorrow.

Part III

The Future

What about the Church of Tomorrow?

Chapter Nine

The Emerging Church

The "**Emerging Church**" (also known as the emerging church movement) is a controversial 21st Century Protestant Christian movement whose participants seek to engage postmodern people, especially the unchurched and post-churched. To accomplish this, "emerging Christians" (also known as "emergents") deconstruct and reconstruct (redefine and alter) Christian beliefs, standards, and methods to accommodate postmodern culture. This accommodation is found largely in this movement's embrace of postmodernism's post foundational epistemology, and pluralistic approach to religion and spirituality. Is this the future of the church or is it just one possibility?

Proponents of this movement call it a "conversation" to emphasize its developing and decentralized nature as well as its emphasis on interfaith dialog rather than verbal evangelism. The predominantly young participants in this movement prefer narrative presentations drawn from their own experiences and biblical narratives over propositional, Bible exposition. Emergents emphasize the subjective over the objective since postmodern epistemology is ultimately destructive of certainty in objective propositions.

The emerging church movement arose as a response to the perceived influence of modernism in Western Christianity. As sociologists noted a cultural shift to postmodern ways of perceiving reality in the late 20th century, some Christians began to advocate changes within the church that corresponded to these cultural shifts. These critics began to assert that the church was culturally bound to modernism and began to challenge the church regarding its use of institutional structures, systematic theology, propositional teaching methods, buildings, attractional understanding of mission (trying to bring people into the church rather than improving their world), official clergy, worship lacking in pre-modern practices such as incense and candles that evoke sacred feelings, and the role conservatives often played in Evangelical politics.

Postmodern epistemology is fundamental to emerging church movement beliefs and emergents have labored to construct a post foundational theology which rejects certainty in favor of a view they describe as more humble in which emergents see their voice as just one among many legitimate, non-dogmatic religious voices that engage in peer-to-peer dialog or "conversation." Emergents believe it is necessary to deconstruct and reconstruct (redefine and reshape) Christianity in order to engage post-Christian Western culture in this two-way conversation rather than proclaim a message that is alien to and unpopular with that culture.

Ambassadors for Christ

II Corinthians 5:19-21

Introduction

This morning I want to speak to you about a very important subject for us who profess and desire to be followers of Jesus Christ. The waters are muddy this morning concerning what it means to be a follower of Jesus. There are theorems, ideas, and proposals concerning our relationship to Jesus that are impeding the cause of Christ around the world and in our own community. There is the idea that being a follower of Jesus is nothing more than a self-improvement program. If you want to lose weight, gain deeper insights, quit smoking, repair your relationships, or win the lottery then you should get connected to Jesus.

To minimize Jesus to simply another self-help guru like Deepak Chopra, Richard Simmons, Oprah Winfrey, or Tony Robbins is one of the most insane decisions that we could ever make. I will guarantee you that if you surrender your life and will to Jesus then your life will change, but it may not change in the way you wanted - it will be far better, far more challenging, than you could ever dream.

What is an Ambassador?

God has given us the task of reconciling people to Him. That is our challenge. That is our privilege. That must be our passion! Paul says that we are Christ's ambassadors. I did a little work this past week and found out what it means to be an ambassador. Webster's definition of the word, "ambassador" is:

- An official envoy; especially: a diplomatic agent of the highest rank accredited to a foreign government or sovereign as the resident representative of his own government or sovereign or appointed for a special and often temporary diplomatic assignment.
- An authorized representative or messenger.

An ambassador has to be a special person because you can only imagine the trouble our country could get in if we had a bunch of renegade ambassadors running around and spouting off things that did not correctly represent the sentiments of our leaders. Ambassadors need to be controlled by those in authority over them. This is no more true for our governmental ambassadors as it is for you and me who are ambassadors of the Kingdom of God.

When an ambassador of the United States goes to a foreign country he or she can act with the full authority of our government in areas where our leader has given them permission. He or she can only speak what they have been given permission to speak. They can only act as they have been instructed to act. They can say nothing more or less than our government allows them to say. An ambassador to China or Russia or any other country is the representative of our country to that land.

The Rights of an Ambassador

Diplomatic immunity is a form of legal immunity and a policy held between governments, which ensures that diplomats are given safe passage and are considered not susceptible to lawsuit or prosecution under the host country's laws (although they can be expelled). It was agreed as international law in the Vienna Convention on Diplomatic Relations (1961), though there is a much longer history in international law. It is possible for the official's home country to waive immunity; this tends to only happen when the individual has committed a serious crime, unconnected with their diplomatic role (as opposed, to, say, allegations of spying), or has witnessed such a crime. Alternatively, the home country may prosecute the individual.

As Diplomats for Christ we understand that while our earthly body may be subject to earthly laws our souls are protected by God. We are not to fear man, but to fear God. In *Matthew 10:28 Jesus says, "And fear not them which kill the body, but are not able to kill the soul; but rather fear him which is able to destroy both soul and body in hell."*

The Embassy

- The place where the ambassador lives and works ("home away from home").

The ground the embassy is built on belongs to the country that sponsors the ambassador. The embassy is a satellite of the country and the same rights of that country are extended to the embassy.

- Our embassy is the church. Jesus told Peter in *Matthew 16:18, "...upon this rock I will build my church; and the gates of hell shall not prevail against it."* There is protection in the church!

Conclusion

You and I are called to be ambassadors to this world for the cause of Christ. At all times and in all situations we are ambassadors. What is our message? What can we say or do? Great question! Let me share with you what Paul wrote to the Corinthians, *"19...for God was in Christ, reconciling the world to himself, not imputing their trespasses unto them; and hath committed unto us the word of reconciliation."*

This is the wonderful message he has given us to tell others. This is our message. God was in Christ reconciling the world to Himself and forgiving our sins through Jesus. What a message! What a charge! People all over the world are hungry for that message my friend. Their hunger is growing by the day while the church sits back and carries on with our little "get togethers" once a week. We need to come together on Sunday to celebrate what God has done throughout the week! There is the whole world that is dying to know the good news that God has come to us in Jesus to forgive us, take us in His arms, cleanse us from our sin, guilt, and shame, and set us back in the world as ambassadors for the Kingdom. That is the message that you and I have been given to offer to our world.

Narrative theology

Narrative explorations of faith, Scripture, and history are emphasized in emerging churches over exegetical and doctrinal approaches such as that found in systematic theology and systematic exegesis, which are often viewed as reductionist. Systematic study is seen as a relic of modernism born out of the view that cross-cultural absolutes could be found. Emergents embrace the postmodern concept that we can only relate the narratives that cause a person or group to believe in the values they do.

The movement publicly advocates ecumenism though they admit to being intolerant of theological conservatives who view the authorial intent in Scripture as having absolute authority for doctrine and practice. Emergents espouse an open, flexible, and subjective view of doctrine in which they embrace a continual reexamination of theology which causes them to see faith as a journey rather than a destination. This is a natural consequence of their rejection of certainty in faith.

Some emerging leaders claim to "hold in tension" even radical differences in doctrines and morals. This openness leads many of them to extend an invitation to "open minded" people of all religions and social backgrounds to contribute to the dialog or conversation. Some emergents see theology as merely an icon pointing to God rather than as a definition of God that has a 1 to 1 correspondence to "what is." For most emergents this means they do not see any doctrinal expositions as definitive.

Your Reasonable Service
Romans 12:1

Introduction

Brothers and Sisters in Christ, how do you enter the house of God? ***Psalms 100:4 says, "Enter into his gates with thanksgiving, and into his courts with praise: be thankful unto him, and bless his name."*** Jesus tells us in ***John 4:24, "God is a Spirit: and they that worship him must worship him in spirit and in truth."***

Sometimes it's not easy to come to church is it? Sometimes it's a struggle to get out of that warm bed knowing you don't have to go to work or go to school. You know that Monday is just around the corner and you want to get a couple more hours of rest. But God told us to remember the Sabbath day and to keep it holy. Therefore we MUST come to church to worship Him! In other words, we must make a sacrifice in coming to church and in our worshipping of Him.
In our text today Paul tells us that it is our duty to live holy before God.

What we are to do?
Romans 12:1a

The duty pressed-to present our bodies a living sacrifice, alluding to the sacrifices under the law, which were presented or set before God at the altar, ready to be offered to him. Your bodies - your whole selves; so expressed because under the law the bodies of beasts were offered in sacrifice, *1 Corinthians 6:20*. Our bodies and spirits are intended. The offering was sacrificed by the priest, but presented by the offerer, who transferred to God all his right, title, and interest in it, by laying his hand on the head of it. Sacrifice is here taken for whatsoever is by God's own appointment dedicated to himself; *1 Peter 2:5*. We are temple, priest, and sacrifice, as Christ was in his peculiar sacrificing, **Romans 12.**

It must be a Free-Will Offering

Presenting them denotes a voluntary act, done by virtue of that absolute despotic power which the will has over the body and all the members of it.

The presenting of the body to God implies not only the avoiding of the sins that are committed with or against the body, but the using of the body as a servant of the soul in the service of God. It is to glorify God with our bodies.

This is to be a **living sacrifice**; not killed, as the sacrifices under the law. A Christian makes his body a sacrifice to God, though he does not give it to be burned. A body sincerely devoted to God is a living sacrifice. A living sacrifice, by way of allusion-that which was dead of itself might not be eaten, much less sacrificed,

- *Deuteronomy 14:2*1; and by ways of opposition - *"The sacrifice was to be slain, but you may be sacrificed, and yet live on"* - an un-bloody sacrifice.

The barbarous heathen sacrificed their children to their idol-gods, not living, but slain sacrifices: but God will have mercy, and not such sacrifice, though life is forfeited to him. A living sacrifice, that is, inspired with the spiritual life of the soul. It is Christ living in the soul by faith that makes the body a living sacrifice, **Galatians 2:20**. Holy love kindles the sacrifices, puts life into the duties, *Romans 6:13*. Alive, that is, to God.

How it is to be v1b

Romans 12:1b

They must be holy. There is a relative holiness in every sacrifice, as dedicated to God. But, besides this, there must be that real holiness which consists in an entire rectitude of heart and life, by which we are conformed in both to the nature and will of God: even our bodies must not be made the instruments of sin and uncleanness, but set apart for God, and put to holy uses, as the vessels of the tabernacle were holy, being devoted to God's service.

It is the soul that is the proper subject of holiness; but a sanctified soul communicates holiness to the body it actuates and animates. That is holy which is according to the will of God.

- They are the temples of the Holy Ghost, *1 Corinthians 6:19*
- Possess the body in sanctification, *1 Thess 4:4-5.*

What it is to be

Romans 12:1c

The great end we should all labor after is to be accepted of the Lord (***2 Corinthians 5:9***), to have him well-pleased with our persons and performances. Now these living sacrifices are acceptable to God; while the sacrifices of the wicked, though fat and costly, are an abomination to the Lord. It is God's great condescension that he will vouchsafe to accept of anything in us; and we can desire no more to make us happy; and, if the presenting of ourselves will but please him, we may easily conclude that we cannot bestow ourselves better.

Conclusion

Why is Paul telling us to do this? Because it is our reasonable service. There is an act of reason in it; for it is the soul that presents the body. Blind devotion, that has ignorance for the mother and nurse of it, is fit to be paid only to those dunghill-gods that have eyes and see not.

Our God must be served in the spirit and with the understanding. There is all the reason in the world for it, and no good reason can possibly be produced against it. Come now, and let us reason together, ***Isaiah 1:18***. God does not impose upon us anything hard or unreasonable, but that which is altogether agreeable to the principles of right reason. The word of God does not leave out the body in holy worship. That service only is acceptable to God which is according to the written word. It must be gospel worship, spiritual worship. That is a reasonable service which we are able and ready to give a reason for, in which we understand ourselves. God deals with us as with rational creatures, and will have us so to deal with him. Thus must the body be presented to God.

It's hard sometimes to worship and praise God, but the Bible tells us to praise Him in all things. When you know Jesus for yourself, you know the sacrifice He made on the cross for us. The sacrifice He made cost Him His life. Because He was obedient to God the Father He rose from the grave on the third day. We are told it is our reasonable service to be a living sacrifice for Him. Can you do it? If you know Jesus as your Lord and Savior you have all the strength and power you need. God bless you.

Postmodern literary theory rejects the referential theory of language. For them, the text takes on a personal meaning as they experience it, but it has no authoritative meaning such as authorial intent to distinguish a right from wrong interpretation. Likewise, emergents allow for a plurality of Scriptural interpretations. The influence of postmodern thinkers such as D. A. Carson is evident in the emerging church movement's approach to interpreting Scripture.

D. A. Carson

According to D.A. Carson, the emerging church movement rose as a protest against the institutional church, modernism and seeker-sensitive churches. It has encouraged evangelicals to take note of cultural trends and has emphasized authenticity among believers. He believes that at the heart of it is the conviction that there are changes in the culture which signal that a new church is emerging. Christian leaders must therefore adapt to this emerging church. Those who fail to do so are blind to the cultural accretions that hide the gospel behind forms of thought and modes of expression that no longer communicate with the new generation, the emerging generation.

Carson adds to this, stating that "Modernism is often pictured as pursuing truth, absolutism, linear thinking, rationalism, certainty, and the cerebral as opposed to the affective which in turn breeds arrogance, inflexibility, a lust to be right, the desire to control.

Postmodernism, by contrast, recognizes how much of what we know is shaped by the culture in which we live, is controlled by emotions and aesthetics and heritage, and in fact can only be intelligently held as part of a common tradition, without overbearing claims to be true or right.

Modernism tries to find unquestioned foundations on which to build the edifice of knowledge and then proceeds with methodological rigor; postmodernism denies that such foundations exist (it is anti-foundational,) and insists that we come to know things in many ways, not a few of them lacking in rigor. Modernism is hard-edged and, in the domain of religion, focuses on truth versus error, right belief, confessionalism; postmodernism is gentle and, in the domain of religion, focuses on relationships, love, shared tradition, integrity in discussion" [12]

In brief, Modernism focused on the ability to know truths absolutely, or in an objective way. Throughout the Postmodern movement, it has been emphasized that each person is affected by their culture or society in such a way that each person cannot be objective about truth.

Carson replies to this notion and notes that they could humbly offer critiques of modernist confessionalism at its best and gratefully acknowledge that many of us are Christians today because our forebears, sustained by grace, were faithful to the gospel. It seems that most EC leaders are quick to judge the Christianity of Modernism, yet were they not addressing their culture in the best way they knew? Were they not faithful to the gospel message? Are not EC leaders addressing *their* culture in new ways? Similar questions are asked by Carson, and he concludes that the unfair and uncalled-for criticism of the Christianity of Modernism must stop.

When Christ returns, how will He find His church? Will it be as He left it or will He find it "emerging"? I believe that this movement is just that, a movement (or "fad") that is gaining popularity. By denying the Scriptures and allowing for personal interpretation, challenging systematic theology, and redefining Christianity, the emerging church movement loses all that makes the church what it is—an assembly of called out, born again, baptized believers.

The Church That Needs a Funeral
Revelation 3:1-6

Introduction

What causes a church to die? We have no control over things that happen after we die, but what about a church dying while we are alive? Not long ago, a tombstone with the church's name on it was put up in front of the building. I guess they must have received a lot of teasing. They moved the tombstone off to the side. What comes to your mind when you think of dead churches? Maybe it's a small group of Christians in an old building. Maybe it's a congregation of mostly older people and no children. Maybe it's a congregation content to stay just the way they are.

Several years ago, a new pastor was called to a spiritually dead church in a small Oklahoma town. They had a nice building equipped with a beautiful worship center, several attractive classrooms, a spacious kitchen area, and a big fellowship hall. In looking over the church records, the new pastor was disappointed by the attendance figures. The Membership Roll included the names of close to 100 people. The new preacher was astonished! More of that story comes a little later.

Three Things about a DEAD Church

A dead church may seem to be doing very well
Revelations 3:1

> *▪1 "And to the angel of the church in Sardis write, 'These things says He who has the seven Spirits of God and the seven stars: "I know your works, that you have a name that you are alive, but you are dead."*

Jesus calls the church at Sardis "dead"! Yet, many people thought it was alive! Had we been alive back then...Sardis would NOT have been a church...we would have considered it a dead church! They seemed to be very much alive! If the Sardis Church were in existence today...We would see their parking lot full every Sunday. Their attendance figures would be very high. Their preacher would be a very young and a popular guy. The church would have many activities going on. **Yet, something has died inside.**

This church at Sardis had reached a state of being DEAD! Jesus is trying to resurrect this church. He tells them, "You need a revival! Arise!"

If they didn't wake up and change, Jesus was ready to give up on them! What happened to them? How can we avoid ending up like them? We don't want to be a dead church! So, how do avoid their fate?

Let's get back to our story about the dead church! The pastor spent the first week calling on as many members as possible.

He invited them to his first Sunday service. However, the effort failed. In spite of many calls, not a single member showed up for worship! So the pastor placed a notice in the local paper stating that since the church was dead, the pastor was going to give it a decent, Christian funeral. The funeral for the church would be held at 2 p.m. on the following Sunday. As you might expect, the newspaper advertisement became the talk of the town. More of that story later!

We need to maintain a high level of commitment

Revelations 3:2

- **"2Be watchful, and strengthen the things which remain, that are ready to die, for I have not found your works perfect before God."**

The congregation at Sardis had begun to poorly prioritize church. They had a priority for work. They had a priority for their family. They had a priority for their close friends. They had a priority for their activities and hobbies. They had a priority for entertainment. Church WASN'T the MOST IMPORTANT part of their lives. It had become one of the least priorities in their lives.

Jesus told Sardis in ***Revelation 3:2 "strengthen the things which remain, that are ready to die, for I have not found your works perfect before God."***

Oh, the church at Sardis was active! Yet, their works were NOT perfect in the sight of God. They had lost their commitment! How committed are you to this church? Are you nearly 100% involved in this church? Has it dropped to 75 to 50% involvement? Is it 20% or even 10% involvement? You might say, "Well, so what if it's just a few of us?" Listen! Apathy toward the church is contagious! The farther along a church is in these stages toward death, the less involved its people are.

The more intense our people are committed -- the less likely we are to be like Sardis. And that commitment has to come from every member here.

Commitment is more than just in attendance! It's **PERSONALLY** making things happen for Jesus. Once upon a time, a preacher in large church asked this question: "How many of you are involved, or want to become involved in some form of ministry for Jesus -- stand up." About 60 percent of the audience stood up. Then the preacher said to those who were still seated: "If you don't intend to get involved with ministry -- when you leave today, don't come back."

Now, you might think that preacher was wrong. I think he was right. There's no excuse for just sitting in church...and not being involved in some form of ministry for Jesus. You may not want to teach a class. You may not want to work with the youth. You may not want to sing in the choir or be an usher. You may not want to plan our special events. However, **all of us have the time to pray**... for your church, your pastor, your deacons, Sunday school teachers, and all our auxiliaries. You can be actively involved in the Prayer Chain. You can represent this church in taking food to the sick. You can represent this church in visiting the nursing homes. You can represent us in sending out cards and little notes. To avoid becoming a dead church, all of us need to devote ourselves to a high level of commitment to Jesus and this church.

Are you interested in the story about this funeral for a church? Morbidly curious, the whole town turned out for the funeral. In front of the pulpit, there was a large casket, surrounded by beautiful flowers. After the eulogy was given, the pastor invited the congregation to come forward and pay their last respects to the dead church. The people arose from their seats, forming a long line to approach the casket. The suspense was intense! What would they see inside this casket? We'll find out what's inside that casket a little later!

All of us must maintain a close walk with Jesus
Revelations 3:4

- *"4You have a few names even in Sardis who have not defiled their garments; and they shall walk with Me in white, for they are worthy."*

The Old Testament tells us about several heroes of the faith. Enoch, Noah, Abraham, Moses, Joshua, just to name a few. Guess what they all had in common. They all walked with God. These were men who had great power, courage & deep spirituality. How was that possible? They spent time with God. They spent so much time with God that they began to think like He did. What was important to God became important to them. That's the kind of "walking with God" is what the deacons and I are supposed to model for you. That's our responsibility.

Remember what Jesus said in *John 15:5?* *"I am the vine, you are the branches. He who abides in Me, and I in him, bears much fruit; for without Me you can do nothing."*

Leaders in the church MUST remain in the vine! They must maintain a close walk with Jesus. Otherwise, they can do NOTHING!

- *Zechariah 4:6 says: 'Not by might nor by power, but by My Spirit,' Says the LORD of hosts."*

Church leaders who don't walk in the Spirit will fail us! The leaders in Dead churches never understand this. To dead church leaders, it's always their church, not God's. Dead church leaders believe, "if anything's going to get done -- it will be by their wisdom and plans, not God's dead church leaders who strive to control things.

To them, "who is in charge" is the most important thing in the church. They've forgotten that the power in church comes from Jesus! Not from their buildings! Not from their committees. Not from their little groups that manipulate the congregation. It's from Jesus alone. Without Jesus flowing through our lives we are useless. Unless we realize that, our church becomes sick and dies! *Jesus said: "... apart from me you can do nothing."*

What's true for the deacons and me...is also true for all of you! If you don't maintain a close relationship with Jesus, your Christian walk with shrivel up and die. You will be removed from the vine. As more and more people drop off the vine, the church will die! Is that what you want to happen here? Well, let's find out how our story today ends!

The line of people began filing by the casket. Each one peered curiously into the open casket, and then quickly turned away with a guilty, sheepish look. What did they see? Inside the casket, tilted at just the right angle was a large mirror. Everyone saw their own reflection in the mirror!

Conclusion

That is still what happens...when people allow Jesus to confront their sinfulness.

- ***James 1:22-24, "But be doers of the word, and not hearers only, deceiving yourselves. 23 For if anyone is a hearer of the word and not a doer, he is like a man observing his natural face in a mirror; 24 for he observes himself, goes away, and immediately forgets what kind of man he was."***
- ***James 2:17, "Thus also faith by itself, if it does not have works, is dead."***

You've heard the word Jesus gave me to preach today! You've looked into the mirror of God's word!! What did you see? Did you see a Christian committed to Jesus and this church...or did you see a person with dead faith?

Jesus calls us to make a choice: to receive Him as our Savior, to let our lives be made whole again by the power of God, and to remain committed to serving Him in His local church. The choice is up to you! When any church dies, the fault lies with the people...not with Jesus!

Live Churches vs. Dead Churches

Live churches constantly change; dead churches resist and refuse change. Live churches love to try; dead churches feel they don't have to. Live churches have youth that are noisy and can't be still, dead churches are very quiet. Live churches have people problems, dead churches float with the current. Live churches need money and take many special offerings, dead churches focus on their savings. Live churches have dirt and garbage; dead churches seem to just fight dust. Live churches are never satisfied and dream of improvement; dead churches tell it like it used to be. Live churches move in faith, dead churches have to see it first. Live churches are filled with givers and doers, dead churches have tippers and dippers. Live churches make mistakes and learn; dead churches have clean stalls. Live churches try and try again; dead churches say we never did it that way before. Live churches reach out to sinners and backsliders with personal evangelization, dead churches are paralyzed and fossilized. Live churches are better, dead churches are BITTER. Live churches are lighthouses in their community; dead churches are 20-watt light bulbs in a refrigerator.

"What kind of church would my church be, if every member were just like me?!"
God bless you!

Chapter Ten

Church Theology

Can one be a Christian and never go to church? To properly answer this question, we need to define what "going to church" is. The Scriptures condemn the pointless practice of going to an institutional assembly for the wrong reasons (***Psalms. 50, Amos 5:21-24***, etc.). Many say they avoid church because they worship God alone, "in their own way." Well, we certainly are not required to worship in the identical manner--besides, there is no one way described in the Bible anyway. ***But one can't really be a Christian alone.***

Christianity, just like Judaism, is ***corporate*** from its very roots. It is absolutely essential for God's children to learn to work and play together in the kingdom, as house church theology places the kingdom both here (in the church) and in the future (in heaven). So there can be no individual Christian, nor can there be a "radio" church Christian, nor even an "Internet" church Christian. Why? Because of the person-to-person relationship that is at the very heart of the doctrine of church.

The house church movement saw the church as having "fallen," and probably would have dated that fall in AD 313, when the Emperor Constantine issued the Edict of Milan which gave Christians tolerance in the Roman Empire. Later, in 380, Christianity became mandatory for Roman citizenship. Many in the institutional church today still regard these events as a great and glorious day for Christ, but the radical reformers saw in it a tremendous evil. Constantine began a process that changed the church from a persecuted minority to the status of royalty. When he summoned the bishops to Nicaea for the First Ecumenical Council in 325, he had them all arrayed in robes of royalty and saw to their comfort as honored guests of state. He doted over the bishops who had suffered crippling injury during the persecutions of Christianity.

It is not hard to see how these bishops saw in this radical change in their social status the very fulfillment of the promises of God--the state would help the church reform the world and then Christ would return to reign.

As it quickly became flooded with unregenerate people, the church was forced to form hierarchical systems like other human organizations and evolved a theology around the "bishop." That is, where the Bishop was, there was the church. God was understood as working through this chain of human power. This idea had its roots not in the Bible, but in Greek philosophy--God was perfect, humanity was corrupt; therefore, the way to build the church is to create a layered organization that increased in purity from the bottom to the top.

Protestants reject this approach in general. Luther spoke of the "priesthood of the believer," rejecting the need for any intermediary between the individual believer and God. The radical reformers accepted this contribution but centered their understanding of their relationship with God on *community,* rather than on the individual. They saw the Protestant model as excessively individualistic. It did not take into account the need for relationships between believers.

Teaching Theology in the Church

In 18th and 19th century America, the church was a powerful force in society. The sermon had implications for how the town was run. Political leaders knew that preachers and their congregations had particular needs which must be attended to, and society at large was impacted.

This century has seen that situation change. Urbanization, population growth, immigration, and growing pluralism have pushed the church from its position of power and leadership. Modern preachers, even the famous ones, preach to too few people to have much impact on the larger society. The change from town to city has seen to that. In the US and Canada, the church is not in charge, and scarcely makes a proper voting bloc.

In the arena of single issue politics, church people have been successful in making their views known, but one wonders how many minds have been changed by the process, and whether the church's position in society has been enhanced, or diminished.

The church must adjust to these changes. It cannot ignore the vast differences between 19th century and almost 21st century America. What is the role of the church in modern society, and is there any theological basis for that role?

Christian doctrine means literally "teaching" or "instruction" and may be defined as the fundamental truths of the Bible arranged in systematic form. Again, may we define a study of doctrine is also called "theology." Theology is also a "treatise or reasoned discourse about God." Theology or doctrine may be described as the science which deals with our knowledge of God and His relations to man. It is a science because it is a systematic and a logical study, arrangement of certified facts. Sometimes doctrine is set forth as a dogma in the church. As a dogma, doctrinal teaching is the church's statement of the truth placed in a church's creed. There must be doctrine for the body of ministry in Christ to know its foundations, teachings, faith, and order.

The 3 Duties of a Christian
Matthew 6: 1-6, 16-18

Introduction

We are going to cover the three things Christians are to do; otherwise we will be in danger of sin. These three things are the great Christian duties, the three foundations of the law by which we honor and serve God. They are:
- Giving, to the needy,
- Prayer, for our souls,
- Fasting, for our bodies.

We will look closely at all three and by the grace of God we will be able to see if we are doing these three things.

Give

Giving is a very important duty of a Christian. **It is mentioned 871 times in the Bible.** When we speak of giving the very first thing we think of is money. Half of the teachings and parables of Jesus Christ was about money. Why? Because Jesus wants us to know that money is a tool for us to bless God and others. Giving is one of our foundations in serving God and our fellow man. We are to give because God first gave to us. *John 3:16, "For God so loved the world, that he gave his only begotten Son, that whosoever believeth in him should not perish, but* *have everlasting life."* We are to give because Christ gave His life for us.

- **Ephesians 5:25, "Husbands love your wives, even as Christ also loved the church, and gave himself for it."**

Now let's see how Christ tells us to give. In *Mark 12:41-44* Jesus and His disciples observe people put money in the church. Listen, *"41 And Jesus sat over against the treasury, and beheld how the people cast money into the treasury: and many that were rich cast in much. 42 And there came a certain poor widow, and she threw in two mites, which make a farthing. 43 And he called unto him his disciples, and saith unto them, Verily I say unto you, That this poor widow hath cast more in, than all they which have cast into the treasury: 44 For all they did cast in of their abundance; but she of her want did cast in all that she had, even all her living."*

In our text Jesus tells the multitude that our giving should be from our hearts and not to impress anyone. The Bible gives us rules on how to give.

- What to do: *Luke 6: 38* tells us that as we give it shall be given back to us with the same measure that we gave.
- Who should give? *Deuteronomy 16:17, "Every man shall give as he is able, according to the blessings of the Lord thy God which he hath given thee."* We are to give according to our income.
- When should we give? *I Corinthians 16:2, "Upon the first day of the week let every one of you lay by him in store, as God hath prospered him, that there be no gatherings when I come."*

- <u>Who to give to?</u> We give to God. ***Malachi 3:10: "Bring ye all the tithes into the storehouse, that there may be meat in mine house, and prove me now herewith, saith the LORD of hosts, if I will not open you the windows of heaven, and pour you out a blessing, that there shall not be room enough to receive it."***

It sad, but not everyone gives. Some are secret about it. They don't want the pastor or the church to know, and then you have those who are bold enough to tell you that they don't give. But they didn't read ***Malachi 3:9***, which says that those who don't are guilty of robbing God and are cursed with a curse.

- <u>How to give?</u> Secretly.

In ***Matthew 6:3*** of our text Jesus tells us not to be boastful in our giving. We are to keep in quiet, not letting those close to us know that we are giving. And in ***II Corinthians 9:7*** we are told to give cheerfully: ***"Every man according as he purposeth in his heart, so let him give; not grudgingly, or of necessity: for God loveth a cheerful giver."***

Pray

Our second duty as a Christian is to pray. **The word pray is used 311 times in the Bible**. Prayer is communication with God. Because God is personal, all people can offer prayers. However, sinners who have not trusted Jesus Christ for their salvation remain alienated from God. So while unbelievers may pray, they do not have the basis for a rewarding fellowship with God. They have not met the conditions laid down in the Bible for effectiveness in prayer. Jesus tells us to ask, seek, and to knock for whatever we want and to do it in His name. In doing so

He will intercede for us to God. We can pray anywhere, home, school, work, and especially at church.

What is supposed to distinguish Christian churches, Christian people, and Christian gatherings is the aroma of prayer. The house is not ours- it is the Father's. The Bible speaks of the need for preaching, music, and the reading of the Word. These are important. But they must not override prayer as the defining mark of God's dwelling. To keep it simple, do this: we know what it means to take a vitamin. When it comes to prayer, take your vitamin "P."

- *1 Thessalonians 5:25* Brethren, pray for us.
- *1 Thessalonians 5:17* Pray without ceasing.
- *Matthew 26:41* Watch and pray.
- *Philippians 4:6* Pray specifically.
- *1 Thess. 5:17, Daniel 6:10* Pray consistently.
- *James 5:16* Pray fervently.

Above all when praying, believe that you will receive that which you pray for. ***James 1:6-8, "6 But let him ask in faith, nothing wavering. For he that wavereth is like a wave of the sea driven with the wind and tossed. 7 For let not that man think that he shall receive any thing of the Lord. 8 A double minded man is unstable in all his ways."***

Jesus tells us in our text that when we pray to pray in secret and not in public using big fancy words designed to win the praise of men.

In ***Luke 13:10-14*** Jesus tells of two men going to pray, a Pharisee and a Publican. The Pharisee uses big boastful words so that those hearing would praise him. The Publican wouldn't even lift his head towards heaven but smote his chest and asked God to forgive him.

Jesus says that the prayer of the Pharisee never left the room while the prayer of the Publican reached heaven. Jesus tells us to pray in our "prayer closet" where there is no one but you and the Lord. Our prayers should be a sincere desire of the heart from the heart. We should not try to pray like someone else, but as we know how. That's why it's important for parents to train their children at an early age how to pray.

Fast

A few years ago I taught a Bible Study lesson on the subject of fasting at a District meeting. I was amazed at the number of people who had not been taught this powerful duty, this powerful tool given to us from God. To fast means to go without food and or water for a certain period of time usually for religious purposes. **It is mentioned 85 times in the Bible.**

In our text beginning with *Matthew 6:16*, Jesus tells us that religious fasting is a duty required of the disciples of Christ, when God, in his providence, calls to it, and when the case of their own souls upon any account requires it; when the bridegroom is taken away, then shall they fast, *Matthew 9:15*.

Fasting is here put last, because it is not so much a duty for its own sake, as a means to dispose us for other duties.

Prayer comes in between almsgiving and fasting, as being the life and soul of both. Christ here speaks especially of private fasts, such as particular persons prescribe to themselves, as free-will offerings, commonly used among the pious Jews; some fasted one day, some two, every week; others seldom, as they saw cause. On those days they did not eat till sunset, and then very sparingly.

The Jewish people knew about fasting, it was something that has always been done, but what Jesus wants us to know is that when you fast do it secretly, not by looking sad faced as the Pharisees would do. They were doing right but for the wrong reasons. Jesus says in **Matthew 3:16** that they have their reward.

When we perform these three duties we unlock tremendous power from heaven. When we give we show God that we are His children sharing with others what He has blessed us with. When we have needs we pray. There are needs that are especially great - obstacles that have a whole different dimension of difficulty about them. SOME things require a specific breakthrough in the heavens - they are spiritual problems, spiritually discerned, and they require spiritual power to break them. And Jesus says that there is a way to obtain the spiritual power to break through such needs - and here is the substance of my message to you today ...**GODLY PRAYER, WITH FASTING, RELEASES BREAKTHROUGH AND SPIRITUAL POWER!**

How important is fasting? Using an NIV version of the Bible read **Matthew 17:20-22. Look at v21. Where is it? Why is it missing?** Because it tells us that Jesus said that some demons, some situations, some problems require prayer and **fasting!** Now Jesus knew this great value of fasting, and it seems that He developed a lifestyle of prayer and fasting. It's clear He'd been fasting prior to this incident with the demon-possessed boy (He cast it out and said the reason He'd been able to was because *"this kind only come out by prayer and fasting"*. What's the implication? Jesus had been fasting.

Jesus was ready for every occasion of life and ministry BECAUSE He developed a lifestyle of prayer with fasting. THERE IS GREAT POWER RELEASED THROUGH THESE PRINCIPLES.
Let me tie this all together for you.

In *Mark 4:20*, *Jesus* says, *"And these are they which are sown on good ground; such as hear the word, and receive it, and bring forth fruit, some thirtyfold, some sixty, and some an hundred."*

The Bible says when you give it shall be given unto you. That's you thirty-fold blessing. When you give and pray you receive your sixty-fold blessing. And when you give, pray and fast, then you open the windows of heaven and receive your hundred-fold blessing! So, if you're not doing your spiritual duties then don't get mad, jealous, or envious of those of us who do!

Conclusion

We now know the three duties of a Christian. We are to give, pray, and fast. When we do these three things secretly, God smiles on us and rewards us openly. Then the world will know that we are the children of God.

Me and My House
Joshua 24:15

INTRODUCTION

My friends, what we need today are for families to get together, have family conversations/discussions. People are lonely and downhearted because nobody in the family wants to listen. They are all busy and they are not sensitive to the situations.

That is why our teenagers nowadays are looking for something outside the family that will fill-in the void that is inside of them… what do we see and read in the newspaper, young boys hooked up on drugs…teenage girls getting pregnant…by who?

We cannot change the fact that according to statistics, US now belongs to the top ten in drugs and abortion. And this is a prevalent practice in our society probably because the very nucleus of this society (the family) is neglected and taken for granted. What is your family doing in this kind of situations?

Again why, not only the breadwinners are busy but also the government pampered so much our children. Yes in some occasions you can impose discipline but is limited because the moment your hands hurt them physically, in a couple of minutes or hours or so… there you go, the best cop in town is knocking on your door and inviting you not to a dinner date but interrogation in the police department.

But, I tell you even if the society or the government fails to accomplish its duties, God will not. We can lean on Him and I will assure you that He is also working non-stop to lead us in the path of perfection.

Joshua penned this deathless statement when he said, ***"But as for me and my house, we will serve the Lord."***

Joshua was right and he made the greatest decision a father could decide for his family... Joshua will never regret his decision that he and his family will serve the Lord God.

I believe one of the reasons why the society has gone astray or lost because the real and true God - Jesus Christ is out of the picture of our life. He is no longer part of the family portrait.

We need to go back to the basic and undo or refresh what was forgotten for a long time...that is, to serve the Lord and teach our children the reward of allowing God to work in our midst. I am very sure that we all have heard the statement; *" the family that prays together stays together."* I am proud to say the this phrase is true to our family because since we learned how to pray- we have a family devotion and we are praying together every morning before our children get on the school bus. Aside from watching movies and football together... add to it the topics about life- its meaning and purpose and most especially spiritual things. We need to start now or it may never happen or it will be too late.

Every day all of us face many decisions that range from trivial to very important ones. When you get up out of the bed in the morning it is a new day that God, Himself has given to you that could possibly have an outcome that can affect the rest of your life. There are those decisions that we make that will affect us in a positive way and in a negative way.

There are two different crossroads that can have the cause and effect syndrome in life. The **positive road** is the road to achieving **Godly success**, and the **negative road** we will classify as **dead end decisions**.

Our text gives us the perfect Biblical example that when we make the wrong decisions it WILL affect us in a negative way. The first cause and effect of a dead end decision is:

- TINY TENDENCIES - The tendency to move, thinks, or act in a particular way.

As we look behind the history of this text when Joshua told the people to choose, it puts into our mind the tendencies that they had with the leader Moses that was before Joshua. At first their tendencies were not that big of a deal. Right? WRONG! Let's look at a few tiny tendencies that they had that caused some dead end decisions to be made.

THE MURMURING (Low indistinct sound)

In the book of *Exodus 16-17,* it gives us a history of the tendencies that the children of Israel had.

- God provided manna from heaven; they enjoyed it for a while and then begin to complain about it.
- God sent them quail from heaven; they enjoyed it for a while and then began to complain about it.
- Then the Bible states that they had a fight with their leader, Moses *in Exodus 17:2* about wanting water. After the meal that God had provided they said to Moses why have you brought us out here in the dessert to die? So, God said to Moses take some

of the leaders and strike the rock at Horeb and water will come out to drink.

The place was called Massah and Meribah because they tested the Lord by saying is the Lord among us or not? <u>Massah</u> means *testing* and <u>Meribah</u> means *quarreling*.

Some people just can't be satisfied. These tiny tendencies of murmuring caused them not to cross over to their inheritance. God told Moses that because of these tendencies they could not cross.

The children of Israel were at a dead end because of a dead end decision! What about you? Do you have any tiny tendencies that are causing dead end decisions in your life? The second cause and effect of a dead end decision is:

TREACHEROUS TRADITIONS
Matthew 15:1-9

What can cause a major dead end decision in our life? Jesus was not just dealing with murmuring and complains but he was dealing with traditions that were taught by men.

Things that are traditional (that we deal with) in the Church that have caused the Church abroad to make bad decisions:
- Church music
- Church (days and times of worship)
- The type of instruments
- The type of music in the Church
- The type of outward appearance of the Church
- The style of the building its self

- The words or phrases we use in the Church. The list goes on and on!

Jesus was dealing with the same Spirit recorded in *Matthew 15:10-11.* Joshua knew that the children of Israel had a tendency to make dead end decisions because of their treacherous traditions. He would have to lead them in a way that he could communicate that God looks at the heart and not the outward! The only way out of traditions is to teach the purpose of them. If the tradition still works and has a defined purpose then it should still be implemented. If it doesn't then it should be trashed and a new fresh new vision is needed! The next cause and effect is what we cannot keep from happening but God CAN heal from:

TRANSFORMING TRAUMAS

The children of Israel did go through some serious looses throughout the years of things, family, friends, etc. that caused them to make dead end decisions. When it seems that our hope is gone we make dead end decisions. The fact is when we are in the worst of traumas we must eventually come out of them so that we can think clearly to make right choices and decisions. There are some Biblical examples of people that went through traumas that did and did not make it:

- Judas did not make it
- Jesus did make it
- Mary the mother of Jesus did make it
- The rich man did not make it.

Traumas can cause anyone to make dead end decisions but we must get through them. The man with no feet thanked God he had legs! All of these things (Tiny Tendencies, Treacherous Traditions, and Transforming Traumas). Can cause dead end decisions.

Joshua stood up as recorded in ***Joshua 24:14-15*** and told them to make the right decision and not dead decisions! The way we make the right decisions in the face of tendencies, traditions and traumas is to accept:

TRIUMPHAL TRUTH

I Corinthians 2:13 States, "This is what we speak, not in words taught us by human wisdom but in words taught by the Spirit, expressing spiritual truths in spiritual words."

The choices that you make such as:
- The choice to be free from the Tiny Tendencies that bind you.
- The choice to know Gods truth instead of the Treacherous Traditions you have been taught.
- The choice to get through the Transforming traumas of life. These choices can only be made through the Triumphal Truth of God's word! Jesus said I AM the way.

Fathers you are being held responsible for your families, especially their spiritual life. *1 Timothy 5:8* says, *" But if any provide not for his own, and especially for those of his own house, he hath denied the faith, and is worse than an infidel."*

An infidel is an unbeliever. We have fathers who take their families to church, drop them off, and the father goes back home. We have fathers who go to one church and their wife and children go to another church and they think everything's all right, but *Jesus* said in *Matthew 12:25, "And Jesus knew their thoughts, and said unto them, Every kingdom divided against itself is brought to desolation; and every city or house divided against itself shall not stand."*

I preached to you before about "The Danger of being Unstable." We have some unstable fathers who will come to church, rededicate their lives to God, and then disappear. They're unstable. We have fathers who say they want the church to grow but only the way they want it to, not anybody else's.

My sisters don't think I've forgotten about you. If you're a single parent it's up to you to declare that as for you and your house you will serve the Lord. God is looking for the men at every church to stand up and be counted. Stand up in your house, stand up in God's house. Fathers, be the Man God created you to be and lead your family in serving God. Be the Man God created you to be and lead your family to Christ! Be like Joshua and declare, *"As for me and my house, we will serve the LORD!"* God bless you!

In Closing

I end this work with the following scenario. This can easily be a typical church service in the not too distant future.

PASTOR: "Praise the Lord!"

CONGREGATION: "Hallelujah!"

PASTOR: "Please log on to the church wi-fi using the password 'Lord2013J316' "

"Will everyone please turn on their tablet, PC, iPad, smart phone, and Kindle Bibles to *1 Corinthians 13:13*. And please switch on your Bluetooth to download the sermon."

P-a-u-s-e......

"Now, let us pray committing this week into God's hands. Open your Apps, BBM, Twitter and Facebook, and chat with God"

S-i-l-e-n-c-e

"As we take up this morninigs'offering, please have your credit and debit cards ready."

"Please use your iPad to make your electronic fund transfers directly to the church account. Or if you prefer, the ushers will circulate mobile card swipe machines among the pews. If you forgot to bring an electronic device, you are directed to computers and laptops at the rear of the church. Those who prefer telephone banking, take out your cellphones to transfer your contributions to the church account."

The holy atmosphere of the Church becomes truly electrified as ALL the smart phones, iPads, PCs and laptops beep and flicker!

Final Blessing and Closing Announcements: "This week's ministry cell meetings will be held on the various Facebook group pages where the usual group chatting takes place. Please log in and don't miss out.
Thursday's Bible study will be held live on Skype at 1900hrs GMT. Please don't miss out. You can follow your Pastor on Twitter this weekend for counseling and prayers. God bless you and have a nice day.!"

Summary

- *"You will receive power when the Holy Spirit comes on you, and you will be my witnesses in Jerusalem, and in all Judea and Samaria, and to the ends of the earth" Acts 1:8.*

These were Jesus' last orders to his disciples before he left the earth. This group of disciples was the beginning of the church. They were not ordered to build buildings, sing hymns, or do any of those other things people expect of Christians. They were ordered to be witnesses, to tell people what they had seen and experienced during their time with Jesus. They weren't ordered to pass on particular doctrine, but to simply witness to what they had seen. In Jewish law a thing could only be proved by the testimony of two or three witnesses. God had come to be with humankind, and the proof was to be given by these witnesses.

The church membership is made up of *Sanctified* believers. To be sanctified means to be called out, separated, set apart. When true believers are in obedience to the Word, they are called out from the world to do the work of God the Father. Those who are true Disciples of Christ know Him as their Lord and humbly submit themselves to His will.

Finally, everyone who is born again is empowered by the Holy Spirit to live their lives for the Master. When the church is made up of church members, the body of Christ grows *"...and the gates of hell shall not prevail against it" Matt. 16:18.*

Works Cited

[1] "What is the Church". Soc.Religion.Christian. 15 May 2008. 15 May 2008
< http://geneva.rutgers.edu/src/christianity/church.html>

[2] "Ecclesia". Wikipedia: The Free Encyclopedia. 27 August 2007. 23 July 2007.
<http://en.wikipedia.org/wiki/Ecclesia_%28Church%29>

[3] "Church History". All About Religion.com. 2002-2007. 18 August 2007.
< http://www.allaboutreligion.org/church-history.htm>

[4] MacArthur, John. The Master's Plan for the Church. Chicago: Moody, 1991. 82-83, 90-92

[5] "The Early Church". Wikipedia: The Free Encyclopedia. 30 September 2007. 29 August 2007.
< http://en.wikipedia.org/wiki/Early_Christianity#Church_Community>

[6] "The Spread of Christianity". 1Way2God.net. 31 July 2009.
<http://www.1way2god.net/story_universalchurch.html>

[7] Piper, John. Brothers, We are NOT Professionals. Nashville: Broadman and Holman, 2001. 2-3

[8] "What is Wrong with the Church today?" Last Days Mystery. info. 12 September 2007. 12 September 2007.
<http://www.lastdaysmystery.info/what_is_wrong_with_the_church.htm>

[9] "The Market Driven Mega Church and its Mission to Accommodate the Un-Churched". Posted by Curtis James.
I Like it Raw. 05 June 2010.
< http://ilikesitraw.com/2010/06/05/the-market-driven-mega-church-and-its-mission-to-accommodate-the-un-churched/>

[10] Wagner, E. Glenn. Escape from Church, Inc. Grand Rapids: Zandervan, 1999. 23-25

[11] "A Brief History of Church Denominations". Religion Facts.com . 2004-2007 28 September 2007.
<http://www.religionfacts.com/christianity/denominations/history.htm#1#1>

[12] "Protestantism". Wikipedia: The Free Encyclopedia. 11 October 2007. 11 October 2007.
<http://en.wikipedia.org/wiki/Protestantism>

[13] "The World Almanac and Book of Facts, 1997, World Almanac Books, Mahwah NJ
<http://www.religioustolerance.org/us_rel2.htm>

[14] Carson D. A. Becoming Conversant with the Emerging Church. Grand Rapids: Zandervan, 2005. 27-29, 64

Rev. Dr. Stan K. McCrary

Biography

Dr. Stanley K McCrary is a 1978 graduate of Pickens County High School of Reform, AL. That same year he joined the United States Navy. While in the Navy he earned an Associate's Degree in Computer Science at San Diego Mesa College in San Diego, CA. He retired in 1998 after proudly serving his country for 20 years in the Submarine Service. He worked in Chicago, IL as a Design Engineer and then on to Atlanta, GA as a mid-level manager for the same company, SBC Telecom.

He returned to the South in 2000 where life is more relaxed and easy going. He was employed at Columbus Air Force Base as a Telecommunications Specialist and then completed a contract job for 4-County Electric Power Association.

In August on 2001 he answered his calling into the ministry. He preached his first sermon and was licensed on Veteran's Day, 2001. In May of 2002 he was called to the Mt Pleasant Baptist Church in Carrollton, AL. He was ordained on his birthday, June 2, and was installed as Pastor in August of the same year.

On July 19, 2008, following the advice of the Apostle Paul; Pastor McCrary continued his studies of God and His Word and earned his PhD (Biblical Studies in Theology) from Masters International School of Divinity in Evansville, IN. In 2012 after four years working as a Configuration/Depot Computer Technician at Logista Solutions in Columbus, MS., Dr McCrary stepped out on faith and began to serve the Lord full time and has not looked back. He continues to faithfully serve as Pastor and Teacher of the Mt Pleasant Baptist Church where he is in his twelfth year. He lives in Steens, MS where he is married to his 1st grade sweetheart Surenell and together they have five children, Marie, LaKiesha, Erica, Xavier, and Kapri.

Dr. Stan McCrary serves as Dean of Christian Education, Lebanon Baptist Association, 2005-Present

Lecturer at the Alabama Baptist Women's State Convention, 2007 – Present

Delivered the opening lecture at the Northwest District Annual Convention in July 2012

Instructor at Ministerial Institute and College, West Point, MS

Co-hosted a daily radio talk show at a Christian radio station, WTWG-1050 AM

Active in state and local politics

Serve on the Board of Directors for Father's Child Ministries

Distinguished Toastmaster (highest level) in Toastmasters International

1st President Columbus Air Force Base Pilot Partner program
Columbus Air Force Base Wingman (#13)

A Blessed Week

May your MONDAY be MARVELOUS
As you start out on your week
May your TUESDAY be TERIFFIC
As you find that in which you seek
May your WEDNESDAY be WONDERFUL
As your weekend comes into view
May your THURSDAY be TRIUMPHFANT
As you know just what to do
May your FRIDAY be FANTASTIC
As you just can't wait
May your SATURDAY be SPECTACULAR
As you rest and rejuvenate
May your SUNDAY be SAINTLY
As you give thanks to your Creator
May your Week be FULL
Of HIS Blessings and HIS Favor

by
Dr. Stan McCrary

www.ingramcontent.com/pod-product-compliance
Lightning Source LLC
Chambersburg PA
CBHW050630300426
44112CB00012B/1736